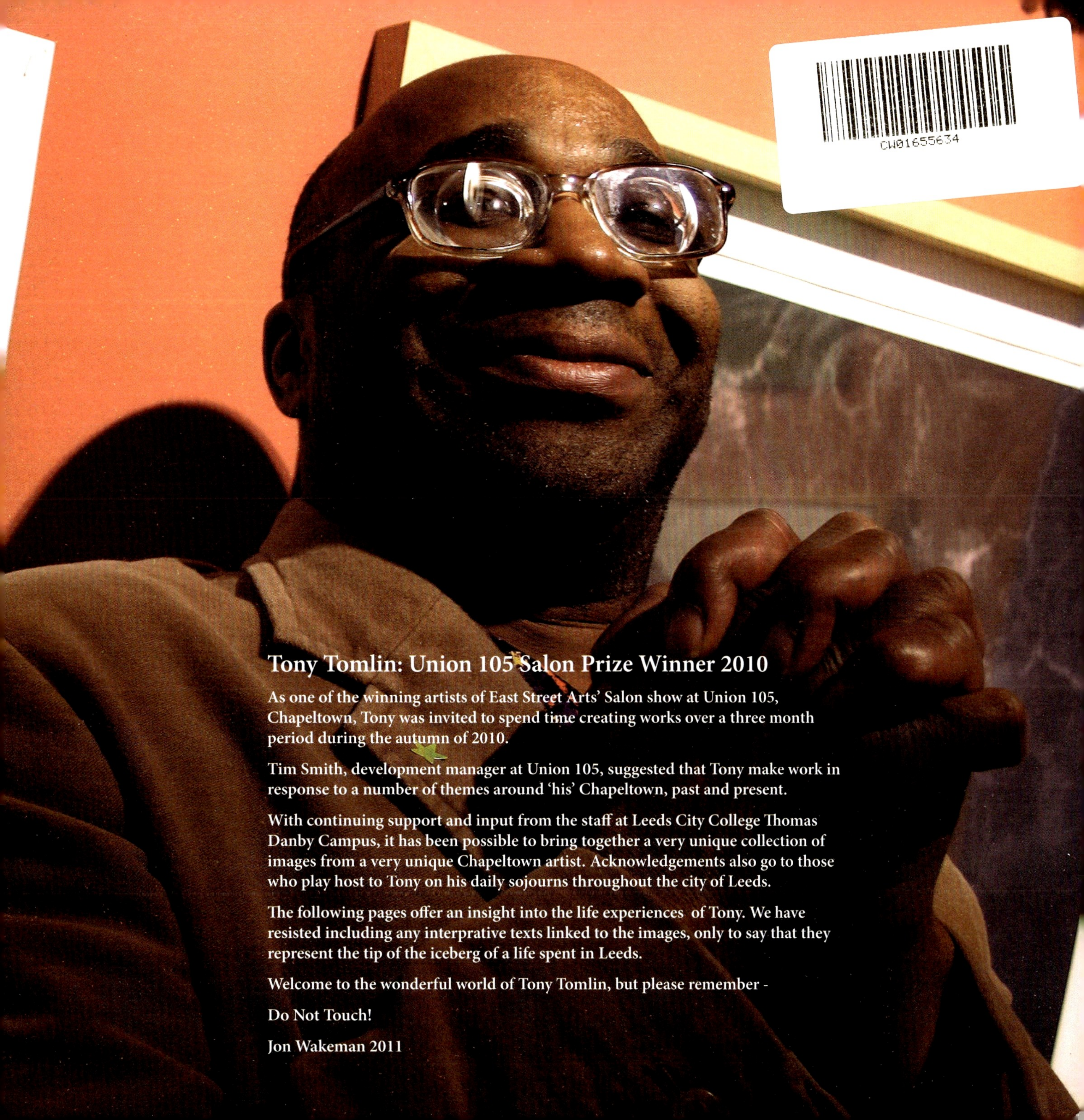

Tony Tomlin: Union 105 Salon Prize Winner 2010

As one of the winning artists of East Street Arts' Salon show at Union 105, Chapeltown, Tony was invited to spend time creating works over a three month period during the autumn of 2010.

Tim Smith, development manager at Union 105, suggested that Tony make work in response to a number of themes around 'his' Chapeltown, past and present.

With continuing support and input from the staff at Leeds City College Thomas Danby Campus, it has been possible to bring together a very unique collection of images from a very unique Chapeltown artist. Acknowledgements also go to those who play host to Tony on his daily sojourns throughout the city of Leeds.

The following pages offer an insight into the life experiences of Tony. We have resisted including any interpretative texts linked to the images, only to say that they represent the tip of the iceberg of a life spent in Leeds.

Welcome to the wonderful world of Tony Tomlin, but please remember -

Do Not Touch!

Jon Wakeman 2011

Do Not Touch Tony Tomlin

ISBN: 978-1-906470-06-7

Published by: East Street Arts . Leeds 2011

Printed in Germany

Design: JWESA

EastStreetArts.org.uk

Union105.org.uk

East Street Arts
Patrick Studios, St Marys Lane, Leeds LS9 7EH

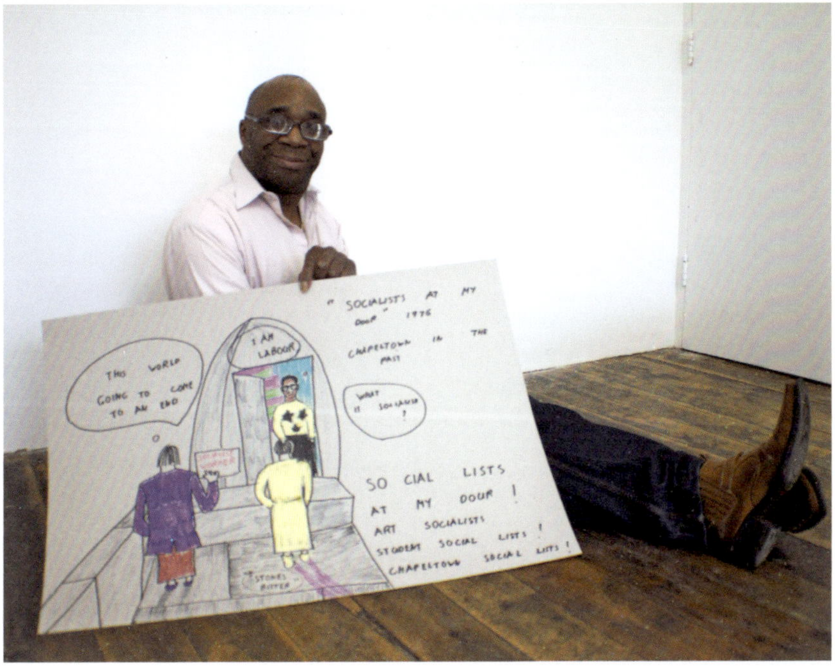

Growing up in Leeds and attending Primrose Hill High School during the early 70s was tinged with a sense of civic pride in the sporting excellence and glamour of Leeds United football team; albeit against a back drop of the gloom of the three day week, power cuts and the National Miner's strike.

A typical day during the long hot summer was a trip to the local church which provided table tennis, snooker, rounders and the odd trip to South Milford. This would be punctuated with classic games such as British Bulldog and football, which would change into a savage game called "Kicks Out" as the evening wore on.

You were expected to be hard and tough and excellent at something in the sporting arena. You were also expected to contribute financially to the family budget as quickly as possible. If either of these characteristics were missing from your personal make up you were considered to be an outsider.

The comprehensive schooling system offered a sure-fire route into the city's vibrant textile and manufacturing industries and, for a lucky few, an alternative route to university.

Very few people chose to go to Art College, especially from Chapeltown. I always remember the firm advice given to Tony by the careers advisor – "There are no jobs in Art son. You would be better off in tailoring."

Joseph Mills 2011

It's a Friday afternoon at Thomas Danby College. The students are thinning out. By four it's more or less empty in the artrooms. Tony, who has been an unofficial 'artist in residence' for nearly 20 years, is sitting working on a discarded piece of greyboard with a cheap yellow ochre oil pastel.

He's been hanging around for an hour or so, back and forth from the college library down the corridor, eagerly waiting for his opportunity to do some work when the formal classes finish.

He has drawn a cluster of cylinder shapes in the middle of the card and written across the top, in smudgy graphite, the word "Jarology".

"That's interesting" I say "What is Jarology?" I know he's deeply religious and I'm ruminating as to whether it's a reference to Rastafarianism or the rapper Ja Rule. Tony looks at me perplexed and then, as if I were an idiot, says noisily in his gruff Yorkshire accent: "It's the study of jars!"

Of course it is.

This is often the danger when interpreting Tony's work; you are tempted by its ambiguity – the open offer of transference - only to be shamed by its frankness. Conversely, the literal reading can also fail; try navigating the quotation, exclamation and question marks and you are equally wide of the mark. Better to yield to the strangeness, enjoy the misspellings, and indulge yourself in the bad puns. Tony doesn't have a sense of humour. It has him.

Tony's technique is beguiling. He is a master of crappy art materials. His use of poster paint, felt tips, cardboard and biro are as accomplished as any craftsman. This is not just necessity. Tutors and friends have given him high quality oils, canvas and pastels over time but he intrinsically understands the qualities of cheap and immediate mark-makers and handles them like a Monet with tube of the finest viridian green oil paint.

It would be convenient to describe Tony as an Outsider Artist. His work has the familiar eccentricity and faux naïve appearance of the untrained, the amateur, or even the savant. In fact, Tony has probably spent more time in educational institutions and art classes than any Royal Academician.

He is known to every art tutor in Leeds. He has enrolled on every level of art course available, from entry to higher education; pre-GCSE to HNC. Yet no course could properly handle him or fully accommodate his commitment to art. He has exhausted them and now he visits like a professor emeritus. He is an Insider Artist. He was the litmus test of a courses efficacy: Could a real artist do this course? What would Picasso get on a Btec? Tony is a real artist and at 50 it is beginning to dawn on him.

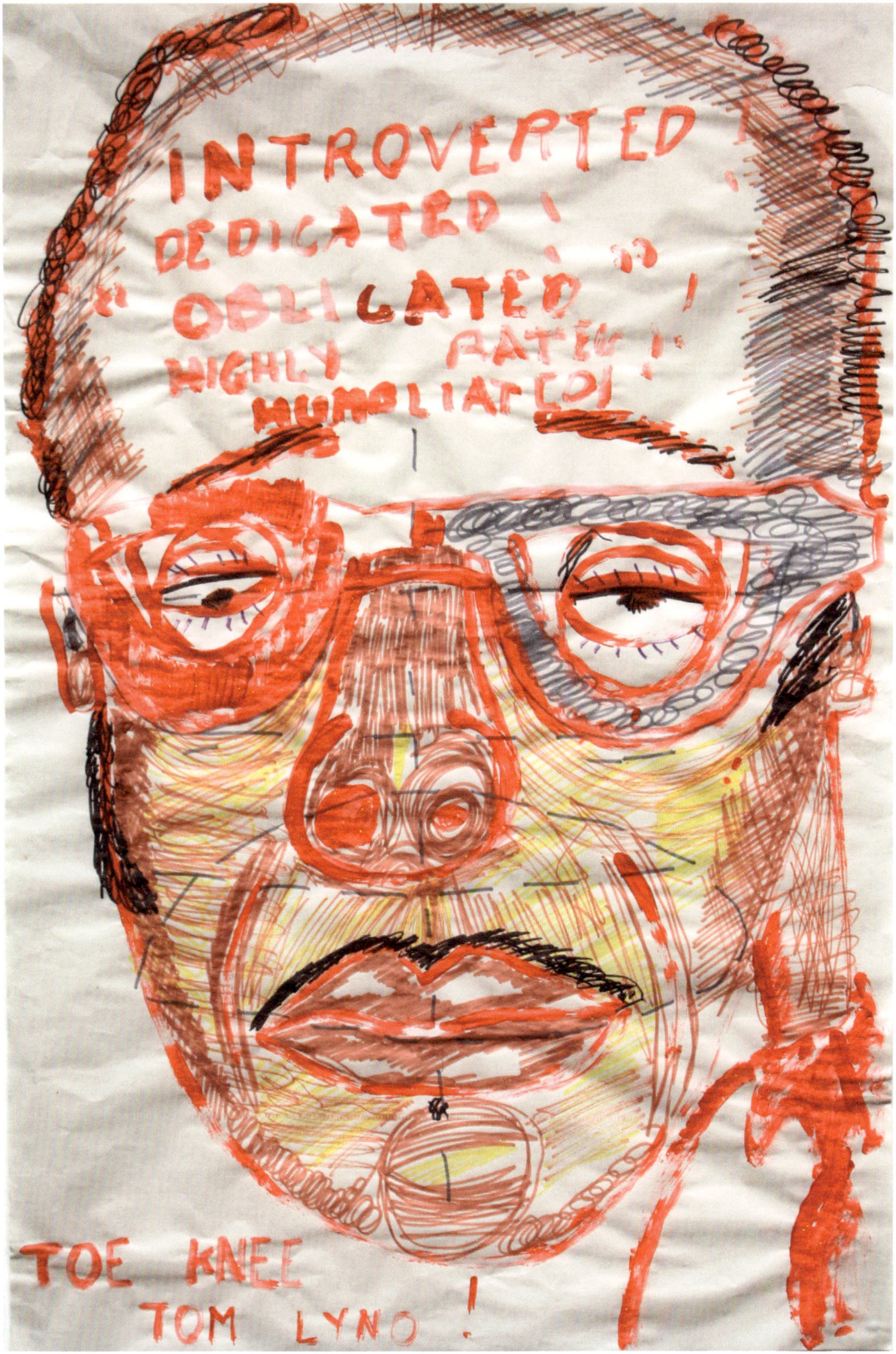
INTROVERTED
DEDICATED
OBLIGATED
HIGHLY RATED
HUMILIATED
TOE KNEE
TOM LYNO !

A cursory description of Tony's day could easily read like a flaneur's in Baudelaire's Paris or an aesthete in Bloomsbury during the first decade of the 20th century. After a trip to the contemporary hair salon and a theological discussion over a coffee at a bar (where all the clientele know him), Tony will begin to consider the day's art practice. Time in the studio with other artists is complemented by visits to the local art college and debate about good and bad art with tutors and students. The day will be finished with further social events and a drink in another hostelry where he will hold forth about humour and painting. Replace North bar with the Colony club, or The Reliance with The Cedar Tavern and you could easily be talking about the life of Francis Bacon or Willem DeKooning. Simply remove the inherited wealth, the fame, the opportunity, the intellectual framework, the status, the narcissism, and there is Tony plodding the streets of Chapeltown looking for a free shave and some company – an audience. His tipple is not Jack Daniels, it's a shandy – "97% lemonade/3% alcohol" neither shaken nor stirred.

Like his daily routine of pit stops to the landmarks that demarcate his world, he returns again and again to the same themes in his work; sex, art, comedy, intelligence, identity, and myopic observational studies. It's a centrifuge with religious epiphany at its core, throwing out a cast of characters that could happily populate Dylan's 'Blonde on Blonde' period.

There are priests, drag queens, personified spoons, food that comes to life, Swedish gigolos, alter-egos (Toe Knees, Sell/wins). His key protagonist of course is Jesus, in all of his contemporary manifestations. Like Mr Benn, J.C. appears as a wrestler, as a cowboy, as Uncle Sam "recruitin' the kids". He sits at card games, roadies at reggae festivals, is an itinerant worker at a circus "erecting" a tent, he plays bass in a Christian hardcore band. He's funked, punked and junked in Tony's mind-blender.

Like an impressionist, Tony 'hits the streets'. He is the lie to Thatcher's No Society and Cameron's Big cynical Society. Everybody loves Tony. He is connected and he connects people. He has put in the miles and stamped out the borders of a village within the city of Leeds. Sometimes he's the village idiot, sometimes the mayor, but mostly he's the town crier. He's loud and he's spreading the word.

Kevin O'Hare 2011

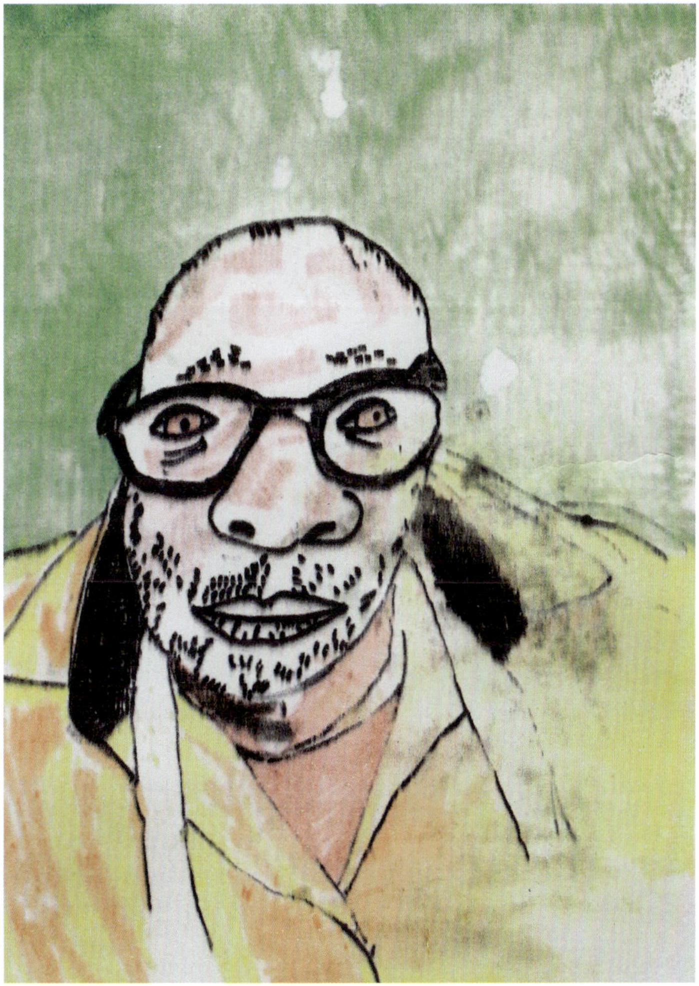

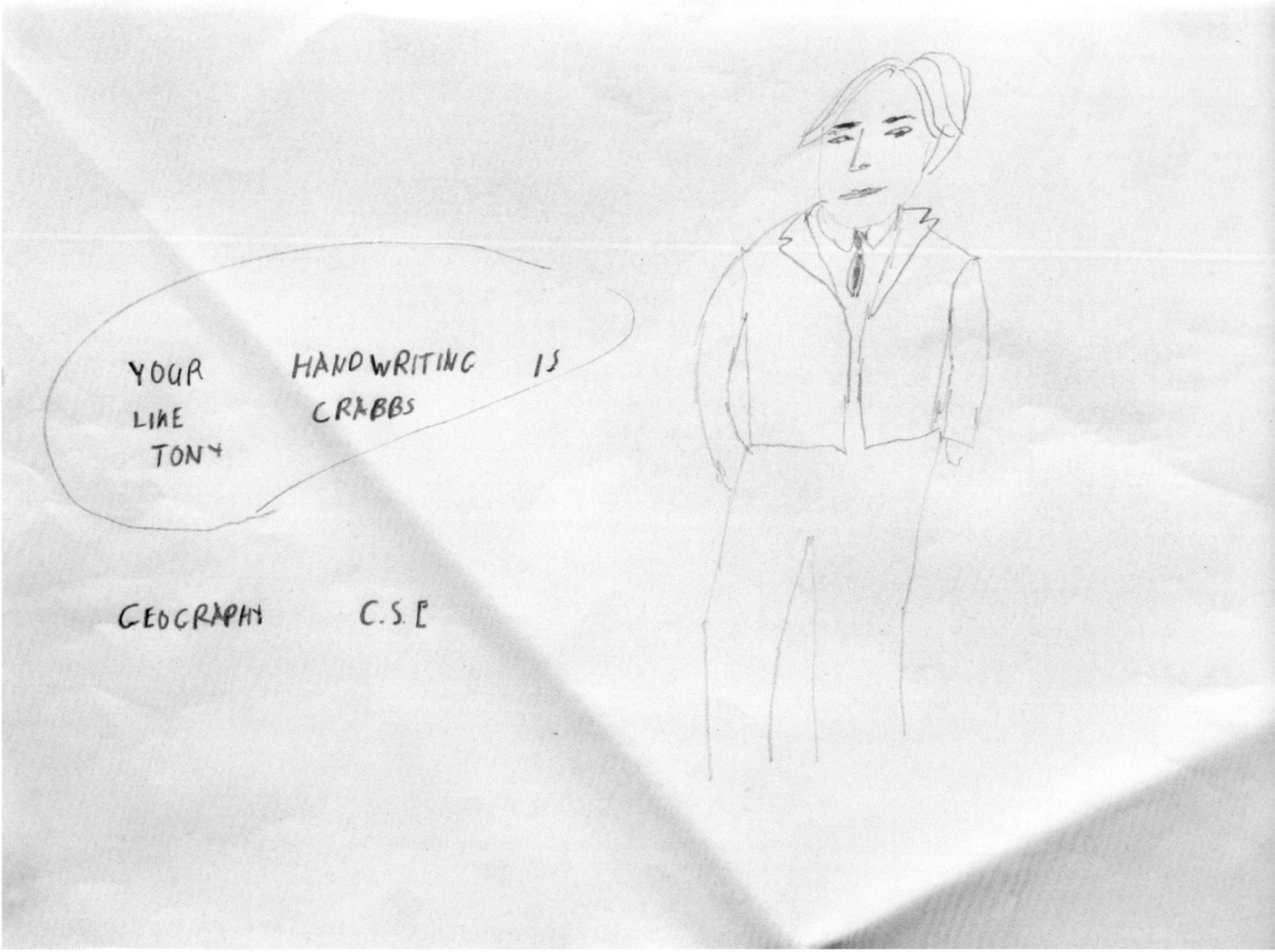
YOUR HANDWRITING IS LIKE TONY CRABBS
GEOGRAPHY C.S.E

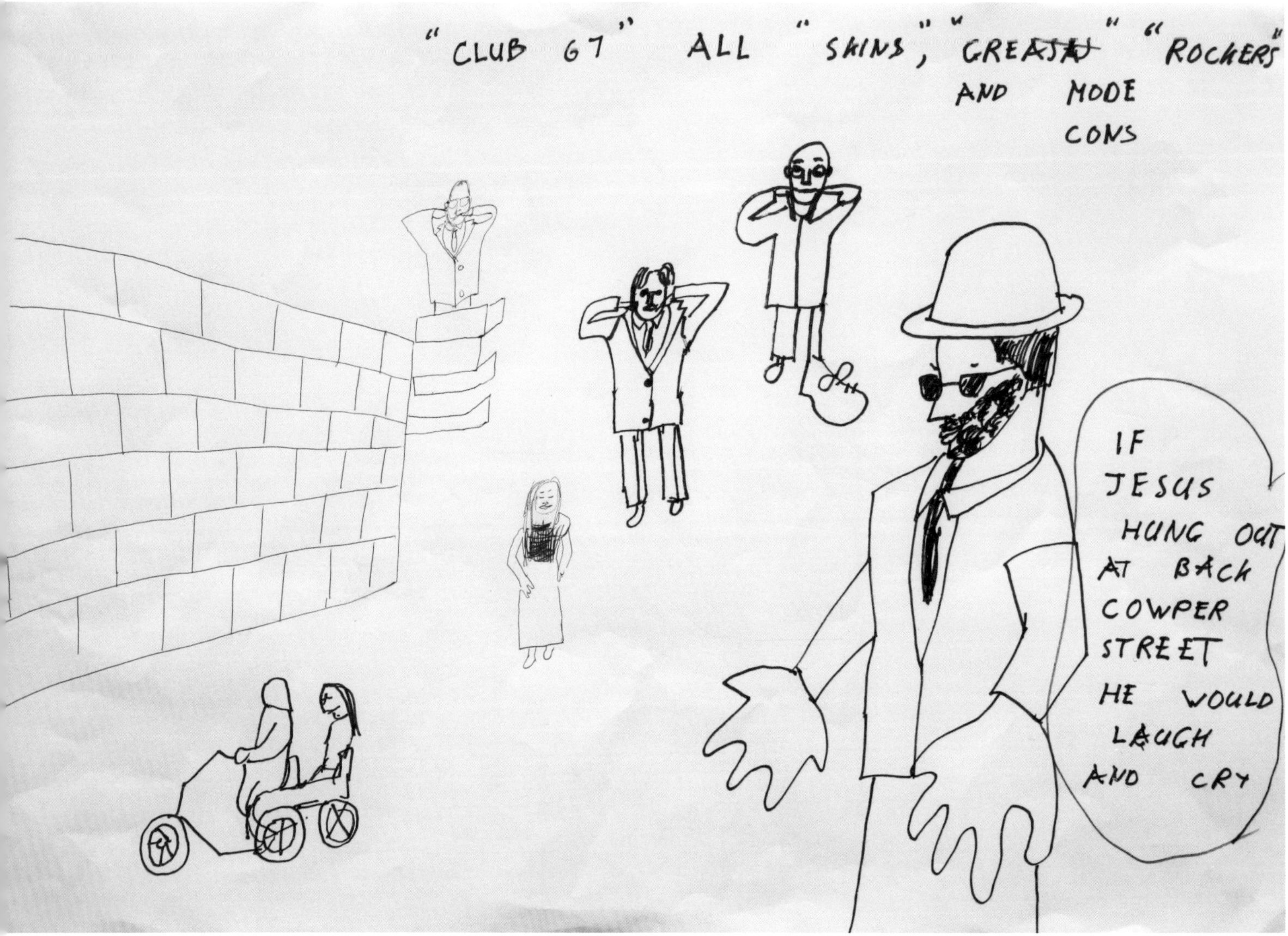
"CLUB 67" ALL "SKINS", "GREASU" "ROCKERS" AND MODE CONS
IF JESUS HUNG OUT AT BACK COWPER STREET HE WOULD LAUGH AND CRY

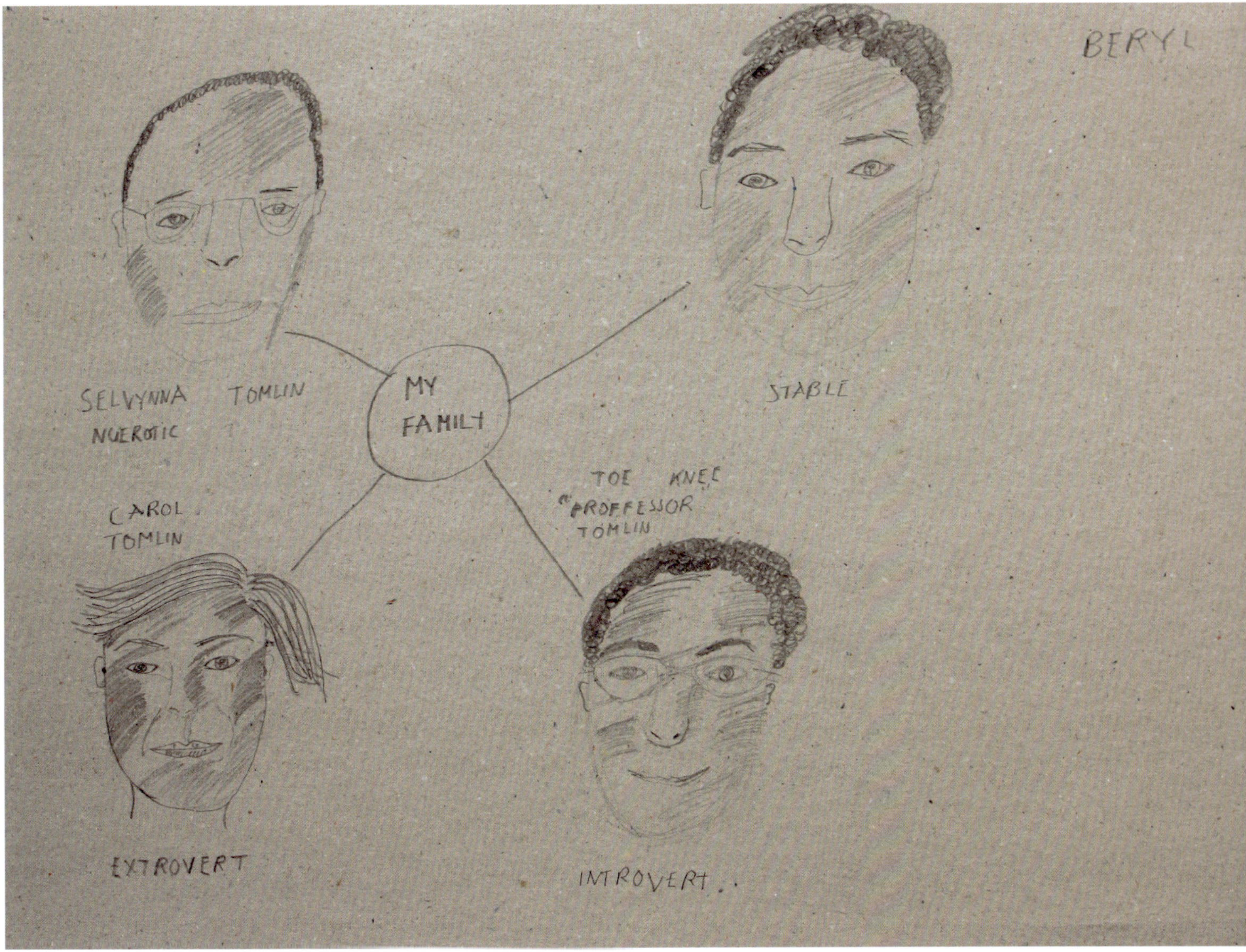
BERYL
SELVYNNA TOMLIN
NUEROTIC
MY FAMILY
STABLE
CAROL TOMLIN
TOE KNEE
"PROFFESSOR
TOMLIN
EXTROVERT
INTROVERT..

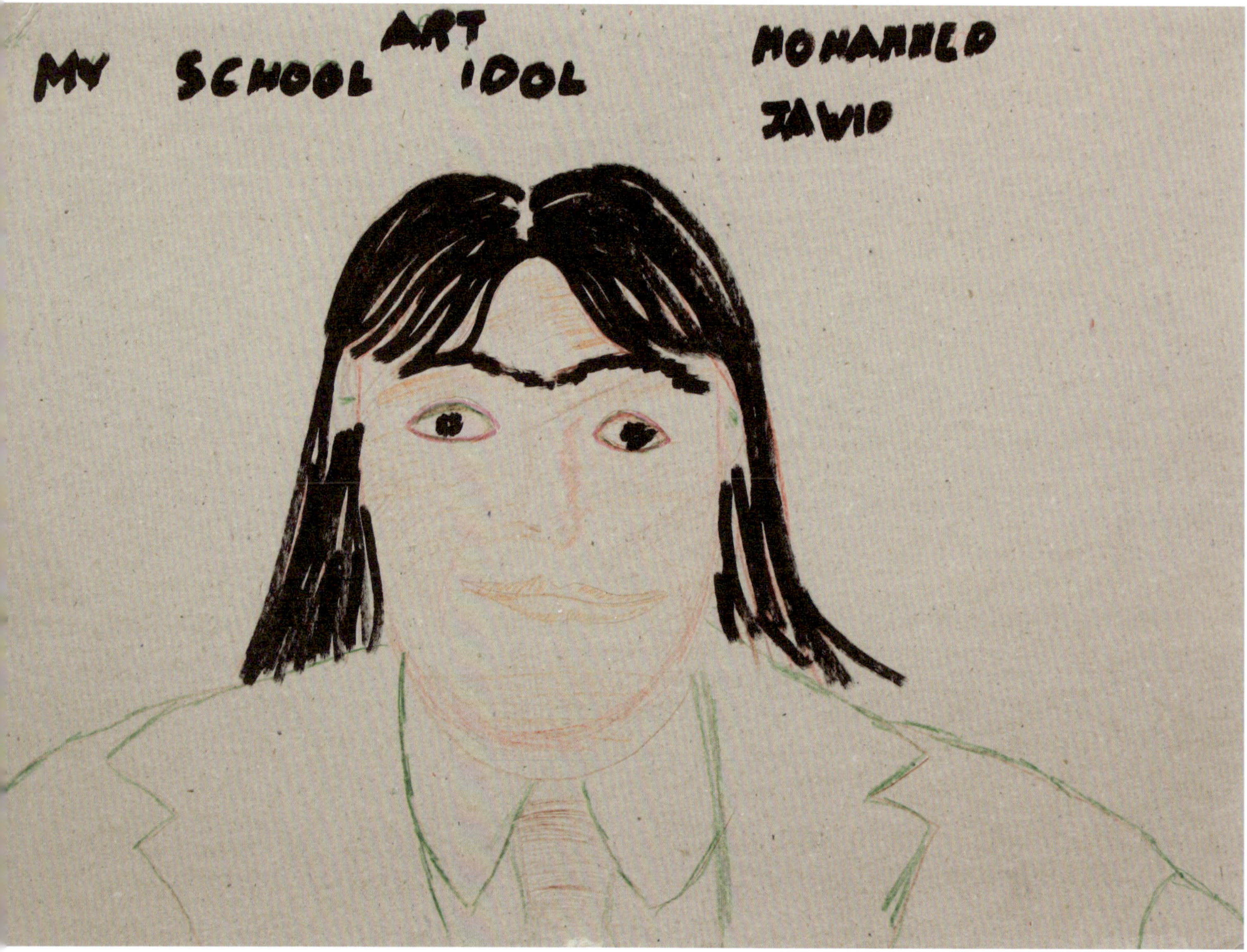
MY SCHOOL ART IDOL
MOHAMMED
JAVID

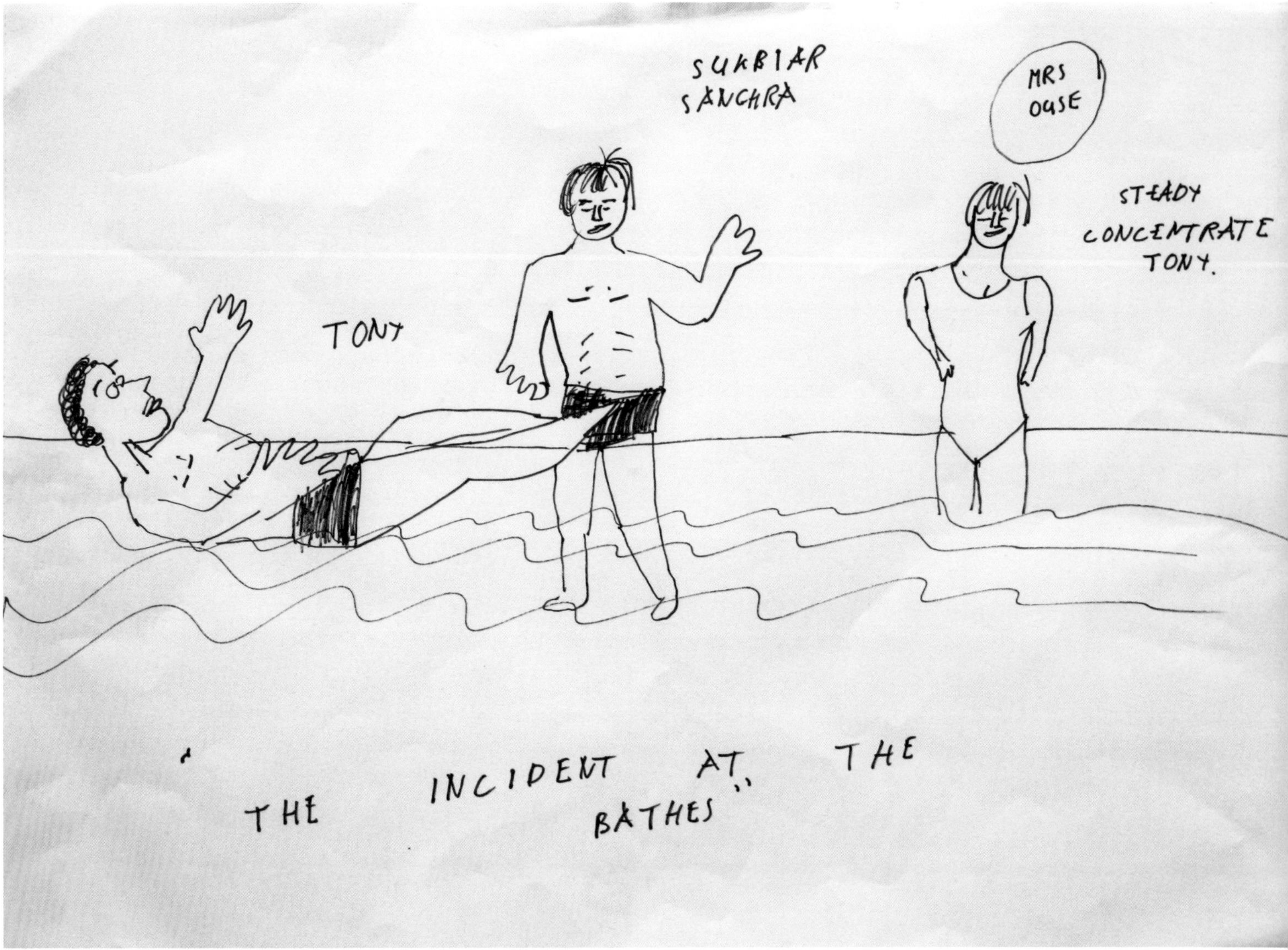
SUKBIAR SANCHRA
MRS OUSE
STEADY CONCENTRATE TONY.
TONY
'THE INCIDENT AT THE BATHES"

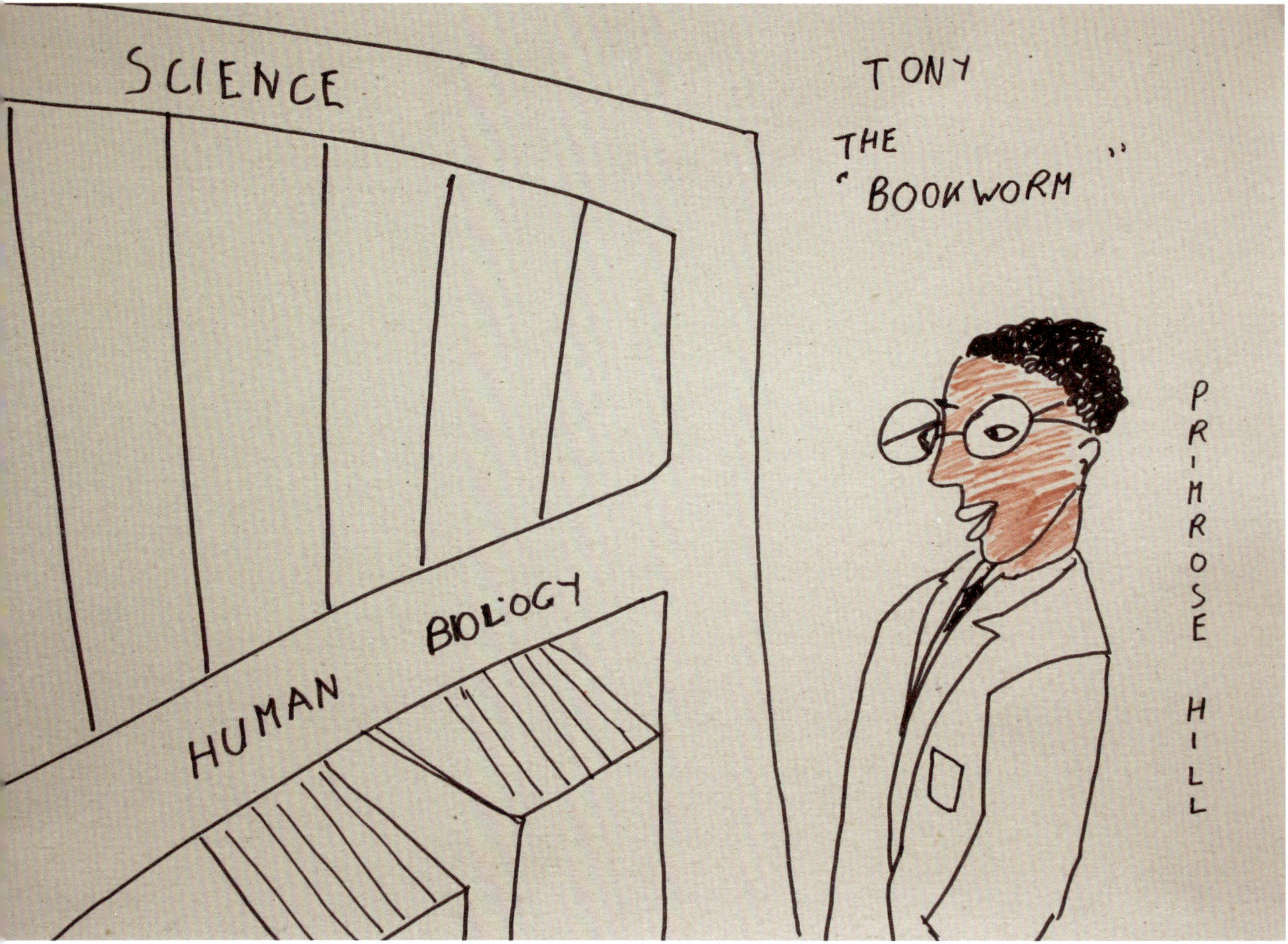
SCIENCE
HUMAN BIOLOGY
TONY
THE "BOOKWORM"
PRIMROSE HILL

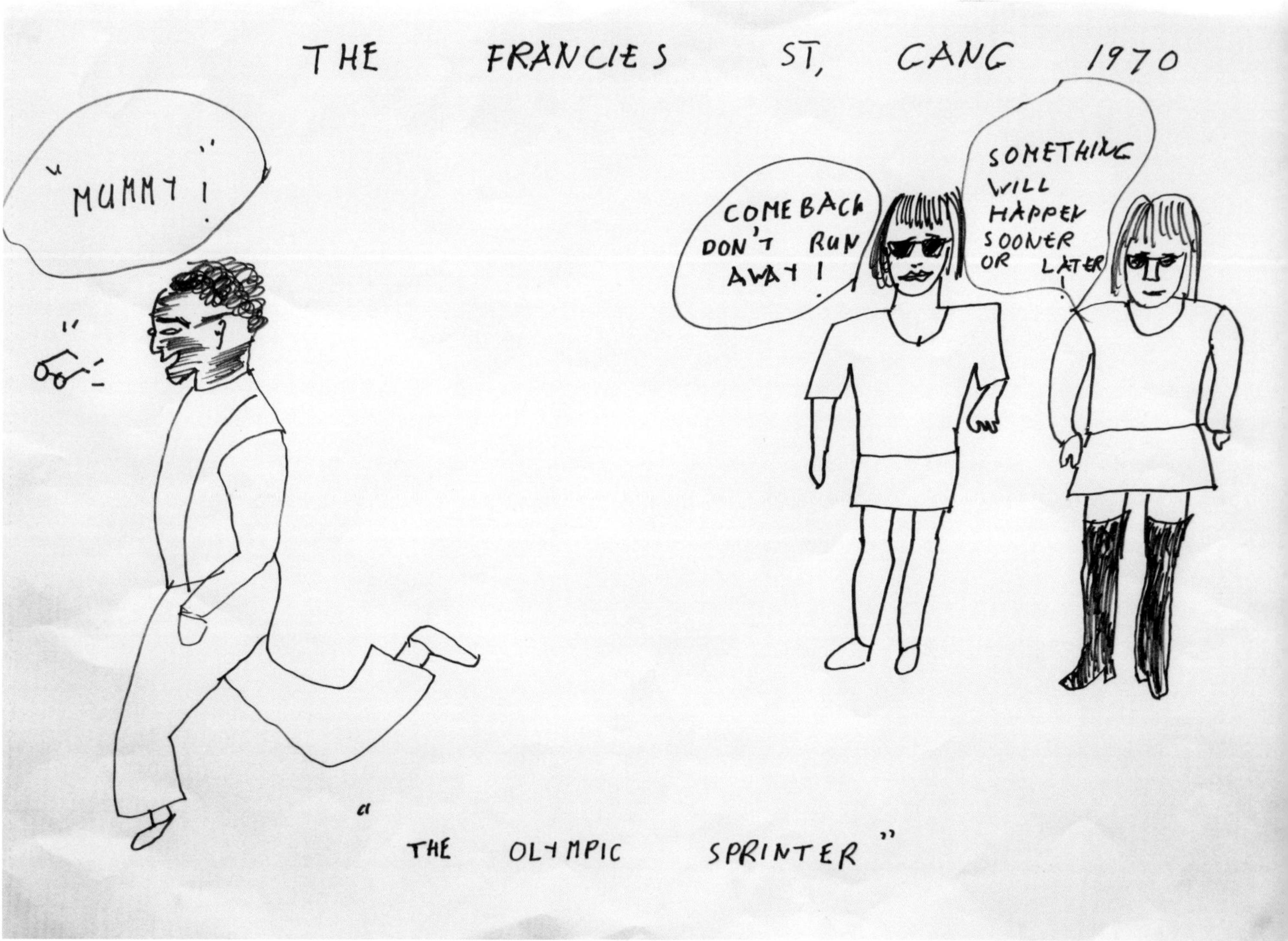
THE FRANCIES ST, GANG 1970
"MUMMY!"
COMEBACK DON'T RUN AWAY!
SOMETHING WILL HAPPEN SOONER OR LATER
"THE OLYMPIC SPRINTER"

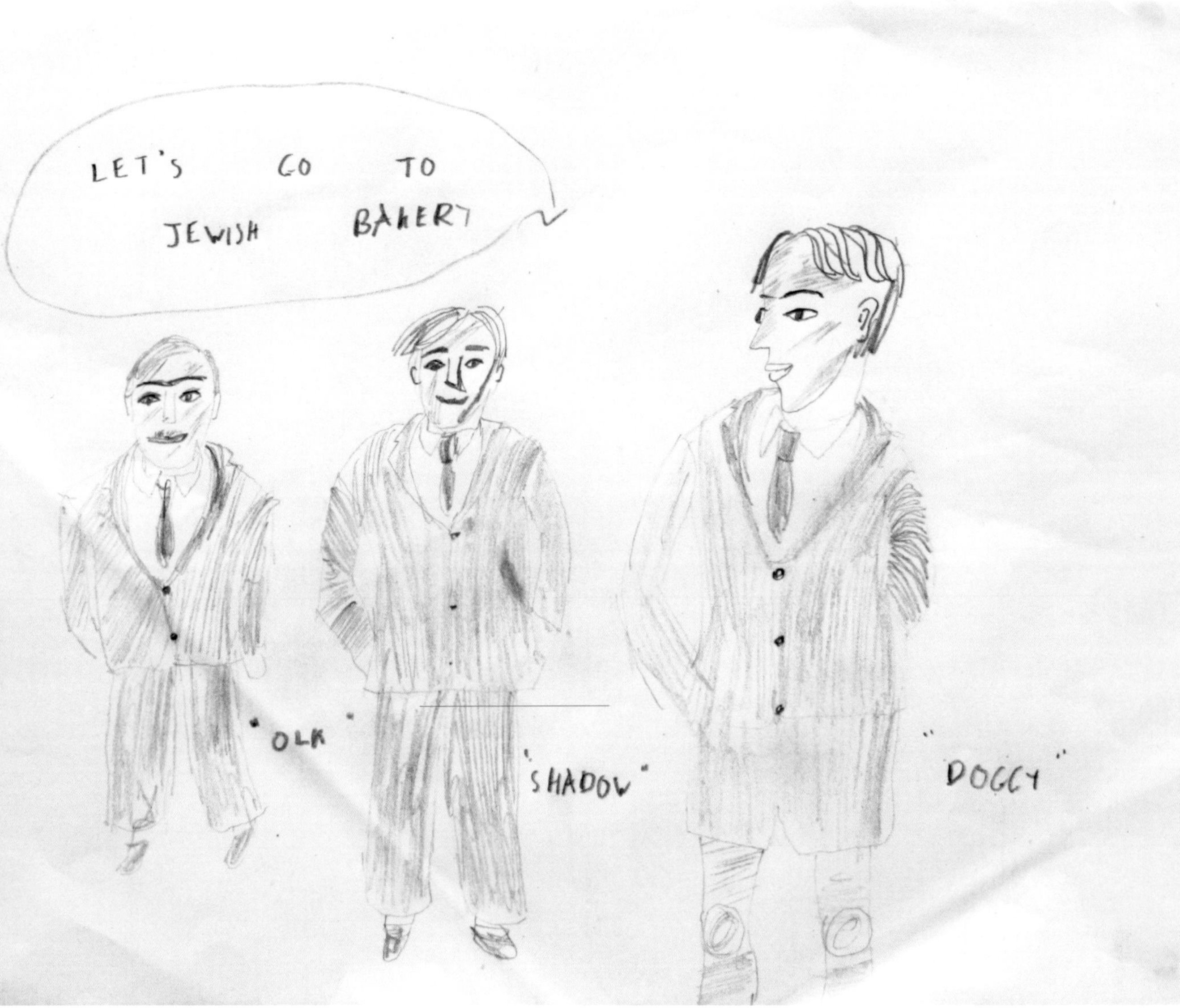
LET'S GO TO JEWISH BAKERY
"OLK"
"SHADOW"
"DOGGY"

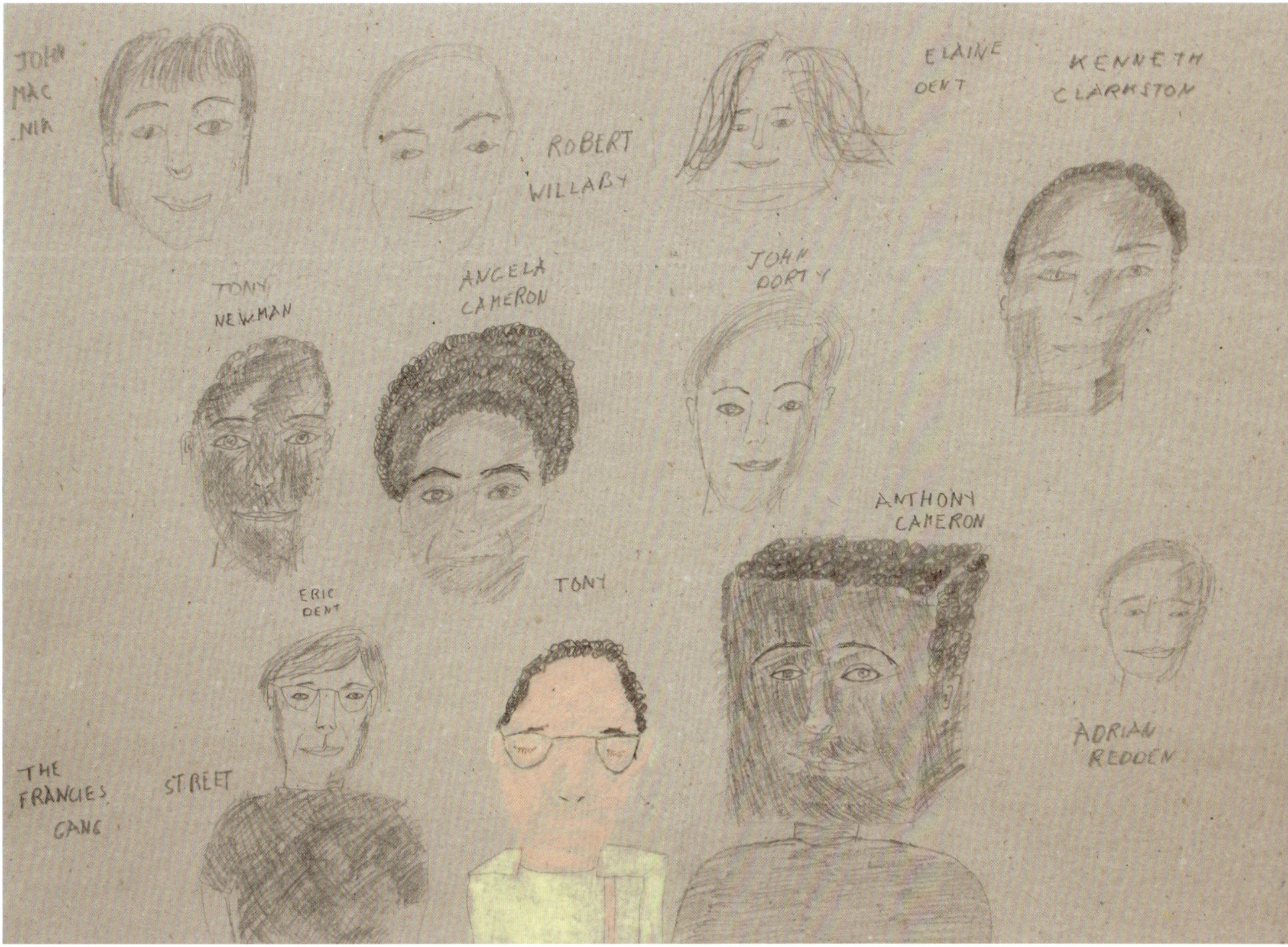
JOHN MAC .NIA
ROBERT WILLABY
ELAINE DENT
KENNETH CLARKSTON
TONY NEWMAN
ANGELA CAMERON
JOHN DORTY
ANTHONY CAMERON
TONY
ERIC DENT
ADRIAN REDDEN
THE FRANCIES STREET GANG

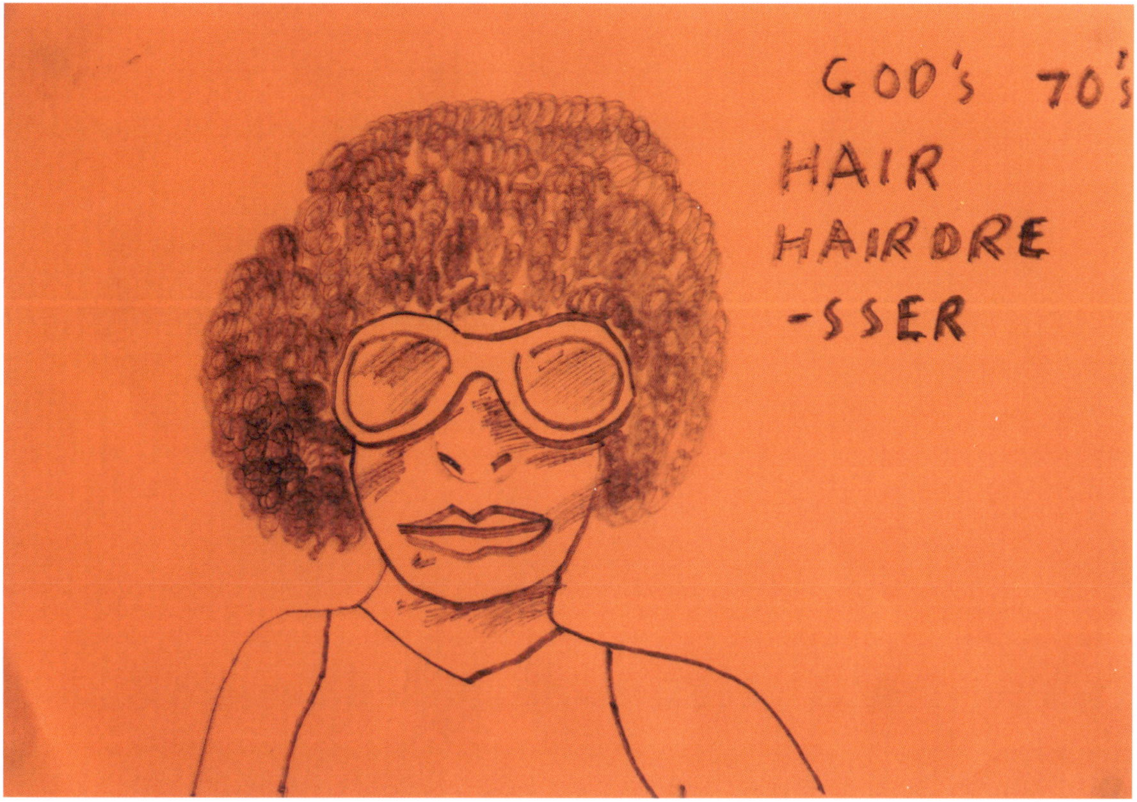
GOD's 70's
HAIR
HAIRDRE
-SSER

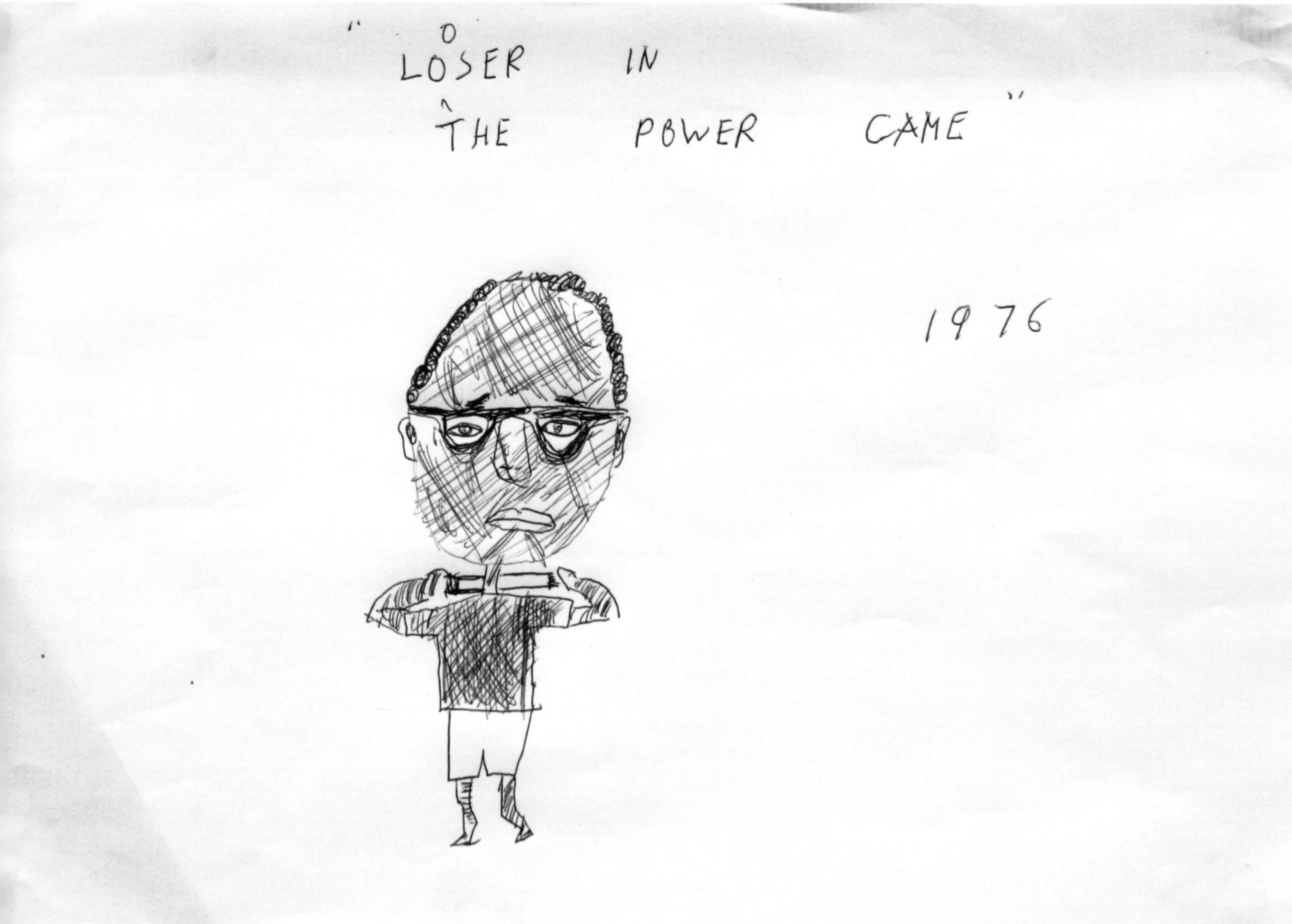
"LOSER IN
THE POWER GAME"
1976

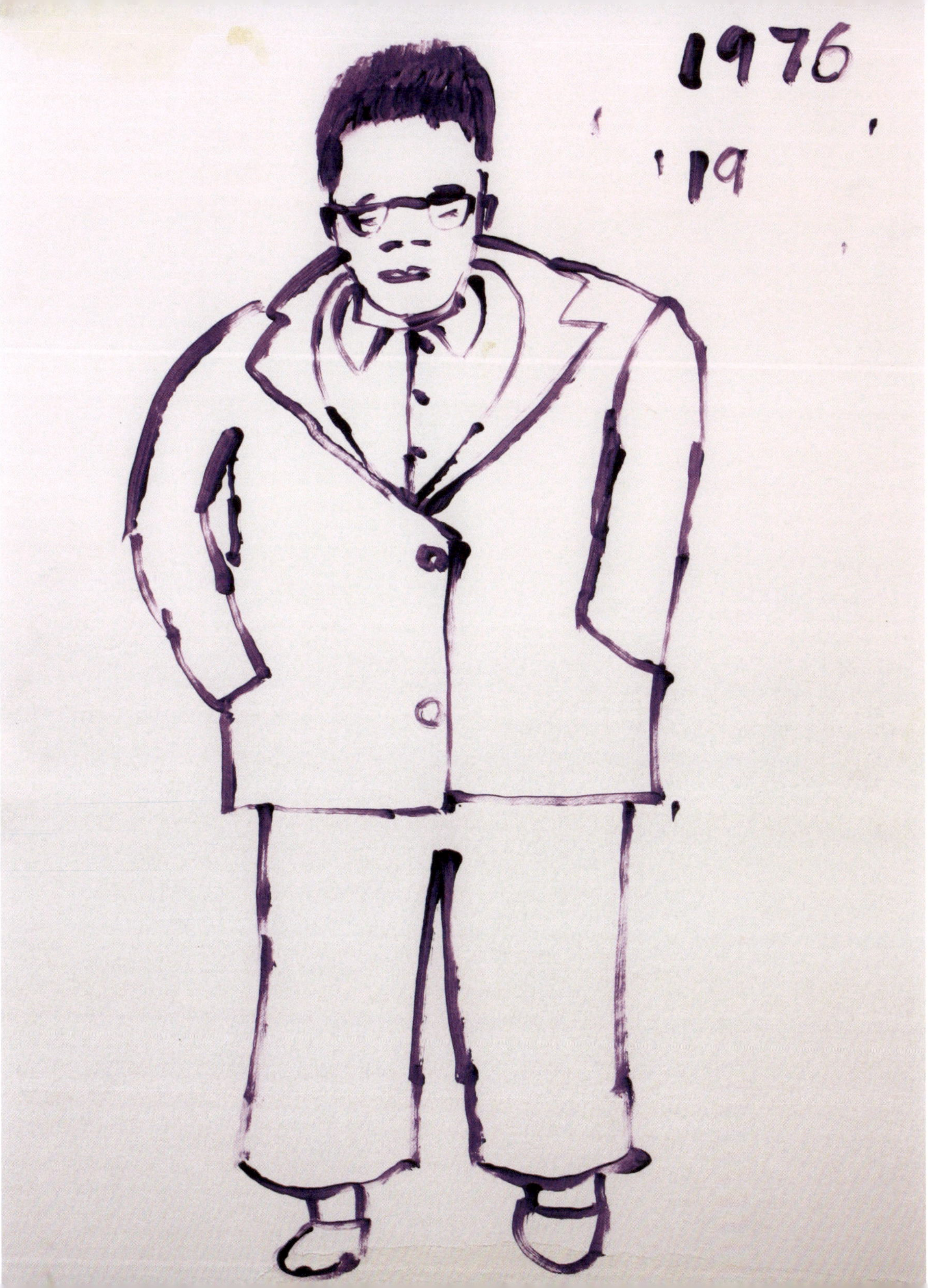
1976
'19

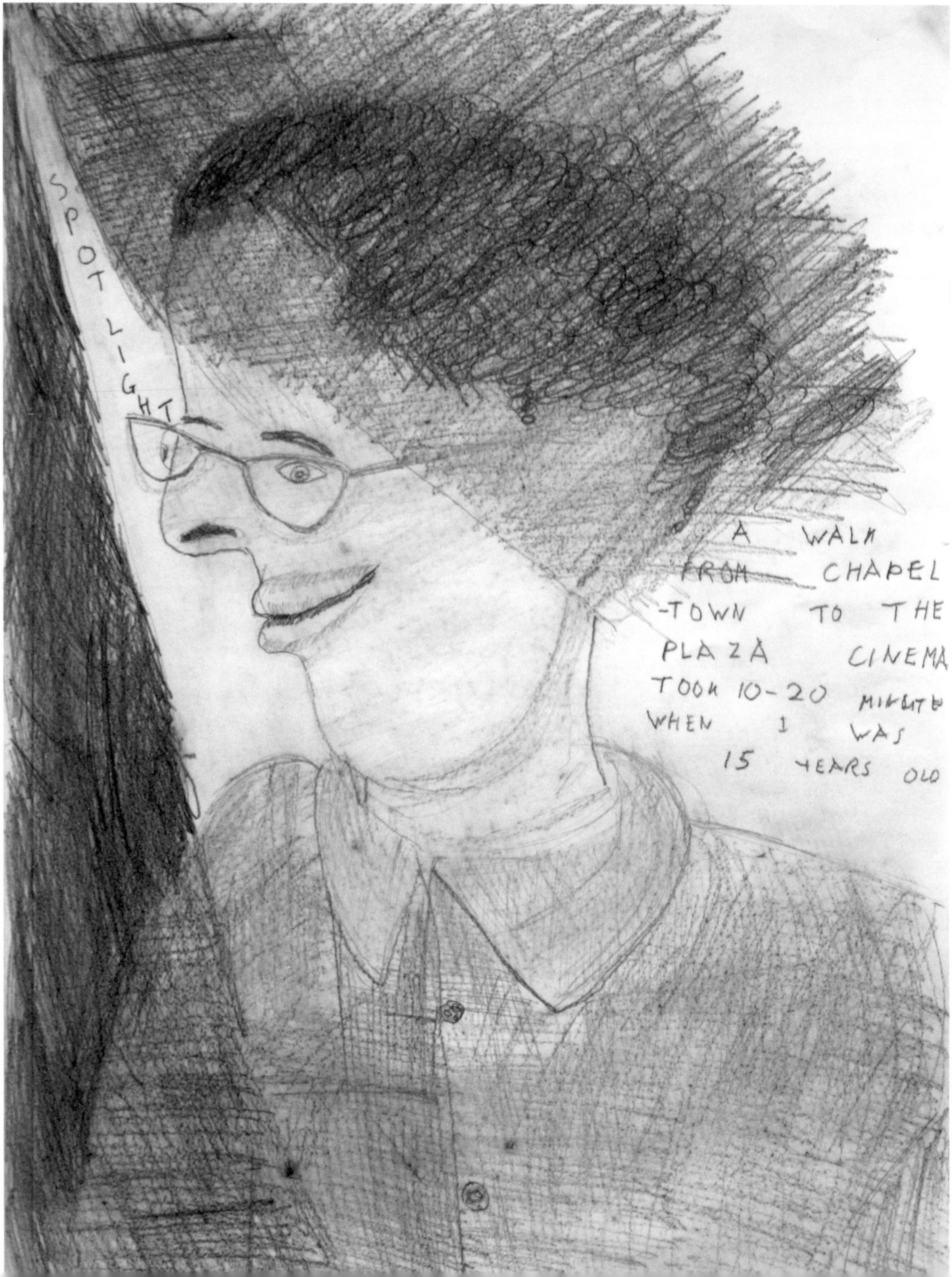
SPOTLIGHT
A WALK FROM CHAPEL
-TOWN TO THE
PLAZA CINEMA
TOOK 10-20 MINUTES
WHEN I WAS
15 YEARS OLD

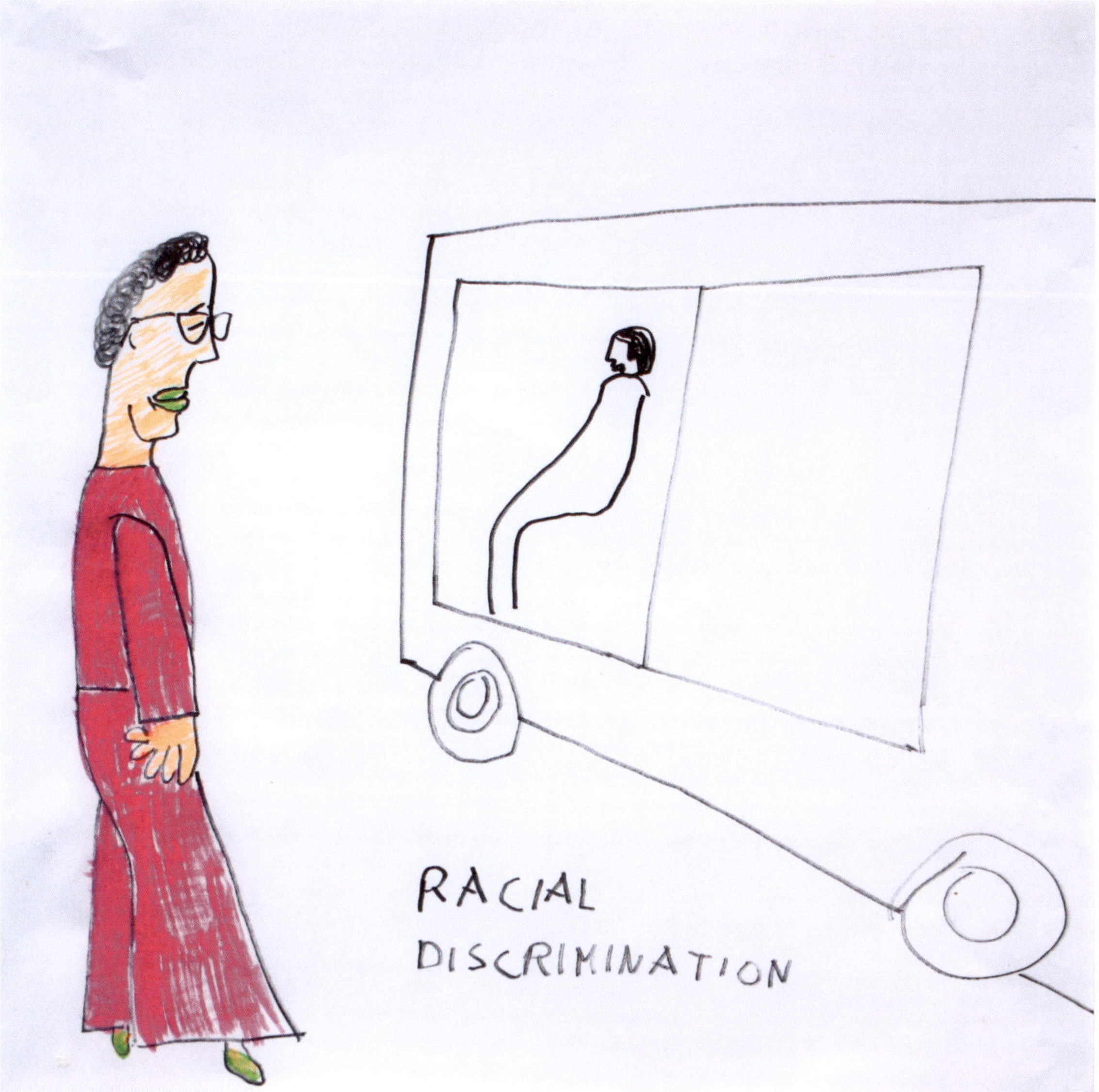
RACIAL
DISCRIMINATION

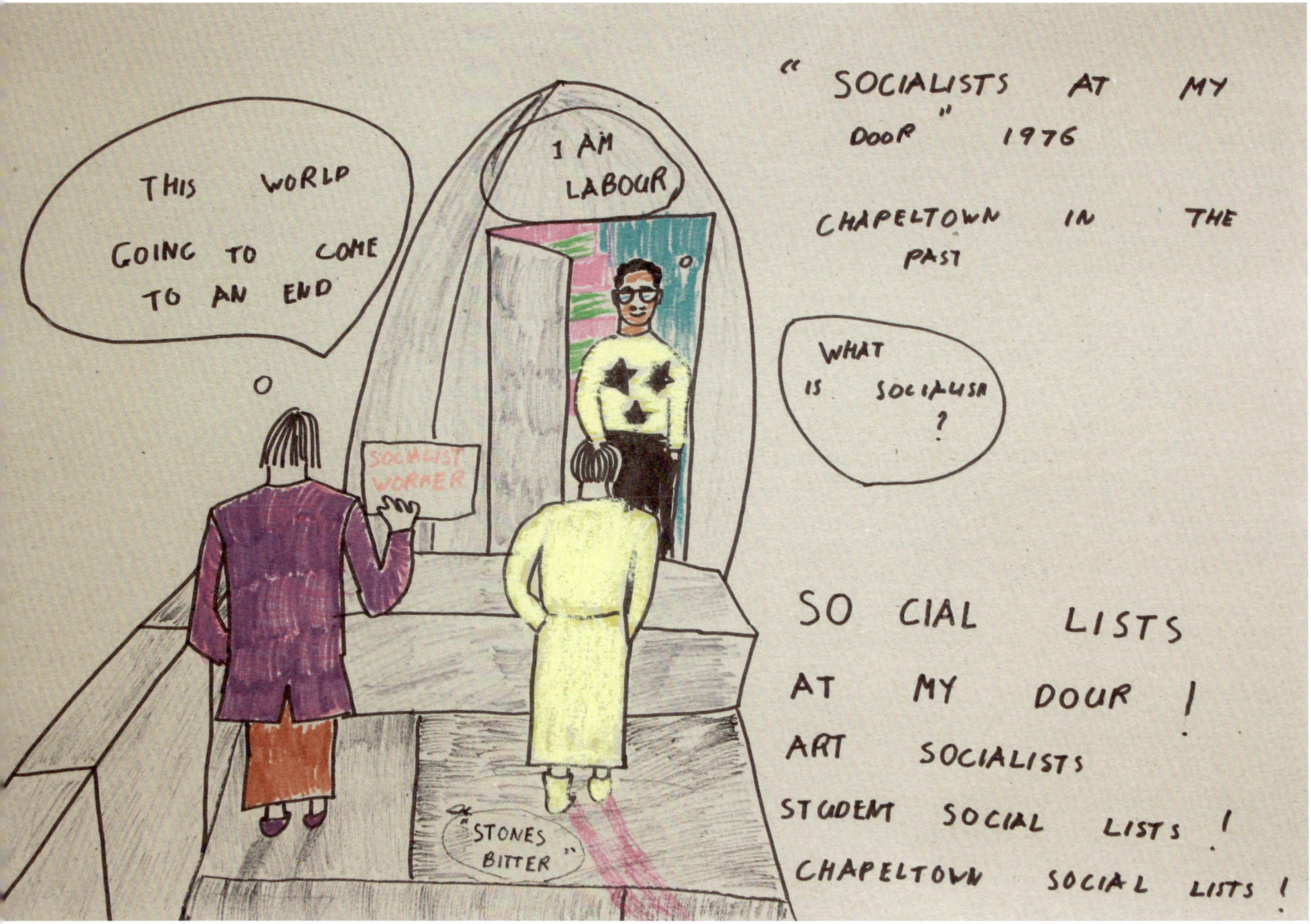

" SOCIALISTS AT MY DOOR " 1976
CHAPELTOWN IN THE PAST
THIS WORLD GOING TO COME TO AN END
I AM LABOUR
WHAT IS SOCIALISM ?
SOCIALIST WORKER
SO CIAL LISTS AT MY DOUR !
ART SOCIALISTS
STUDENT SOCIAL LISTS !
CHAPELTOWN SOCIAL LISTS !
"STONES BITTER"

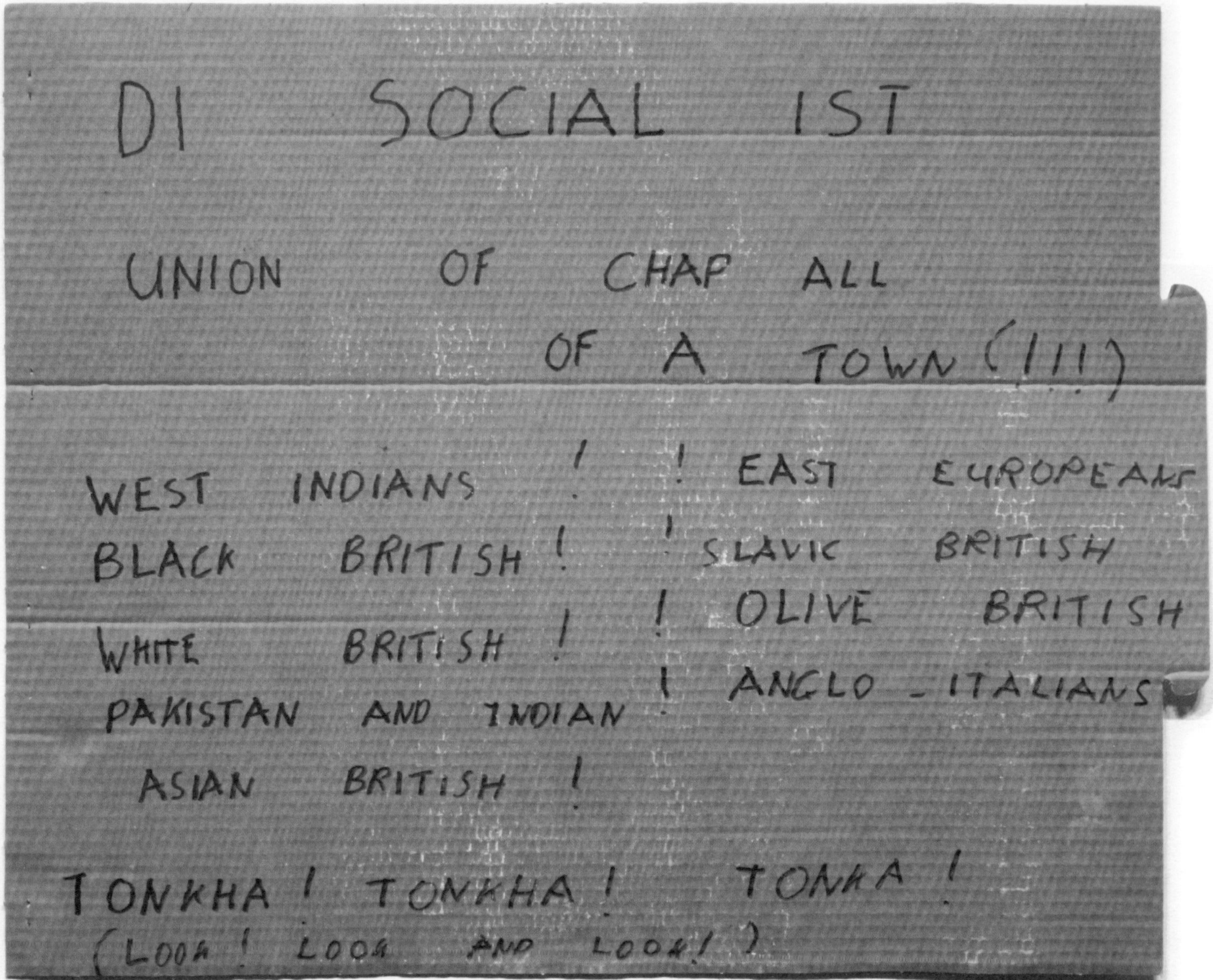
DI SOCIAL IST
UNION OF CHAP ALL
OF A TOWN (!!!)
WEST INDIANS !
BLACK BRITISH !
WHITE BRITISH !
PAKISTAN AND INDIAN
ASIAN BRITISH !
! EAST EUROPEANS
! SLAVIC BRITISH
! OLIVE BRITISH
! ANGLO - ITALIANS
TONKHA ! TONKHA ! TONKA !
(LOOK ! LOOK AND LOOK !)

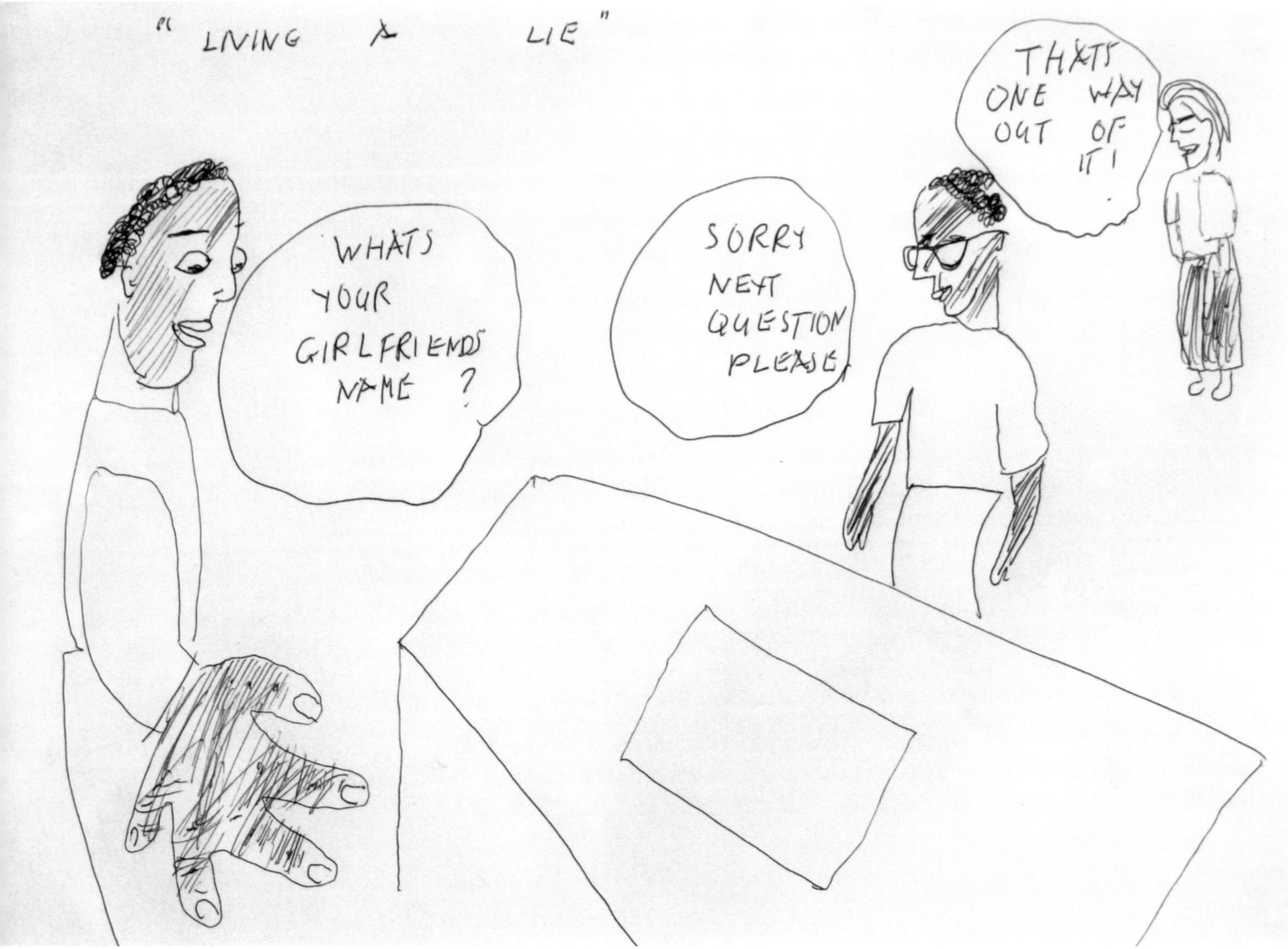
"LIVING A LIE"
WHATS YOUR GIRLFRIENDS NAME ?
SORRY NEXT QUESTION PLEASE,
THATS ONE WAY OUT OF IT!

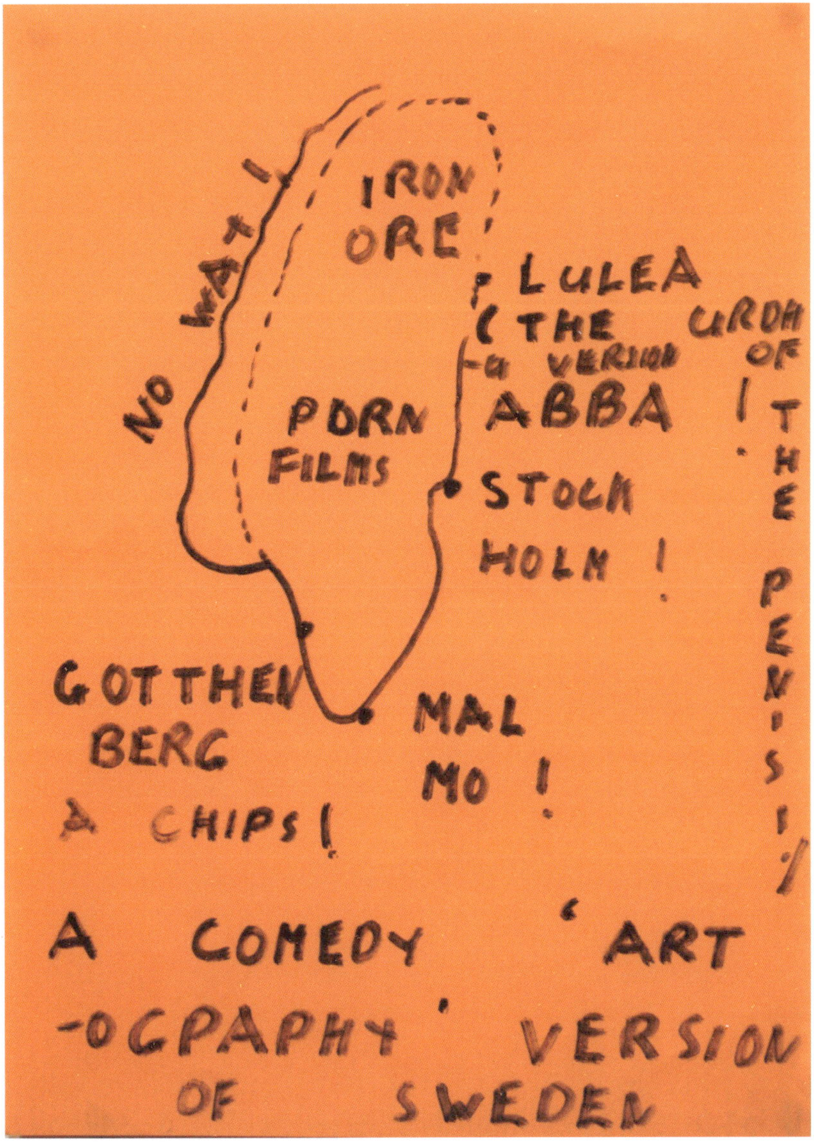
NO WAY!
IRON ORE
LULEA
(THE CURDH
-A VERSION OF
ABBA !
THE PENIS!/
PORN FILMS
STOCK HOLM !
GOTTHEN BERG
A CHIPS !
MAL MO !
A COMEDY 'ART -OGPAPHY' VERSION OF SWEDEN

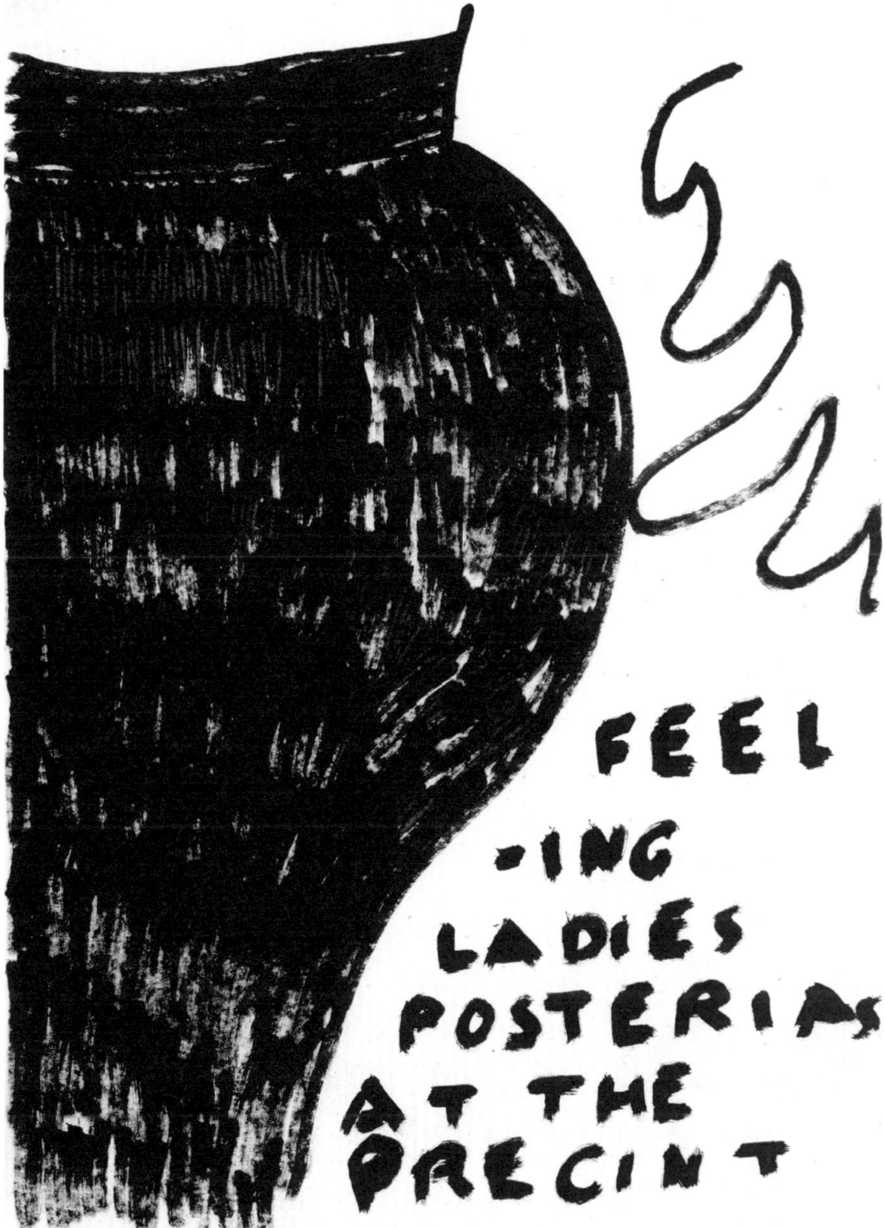
FEEL
-ING
LADIES
POSTERIAS
AT THE
PRECINT

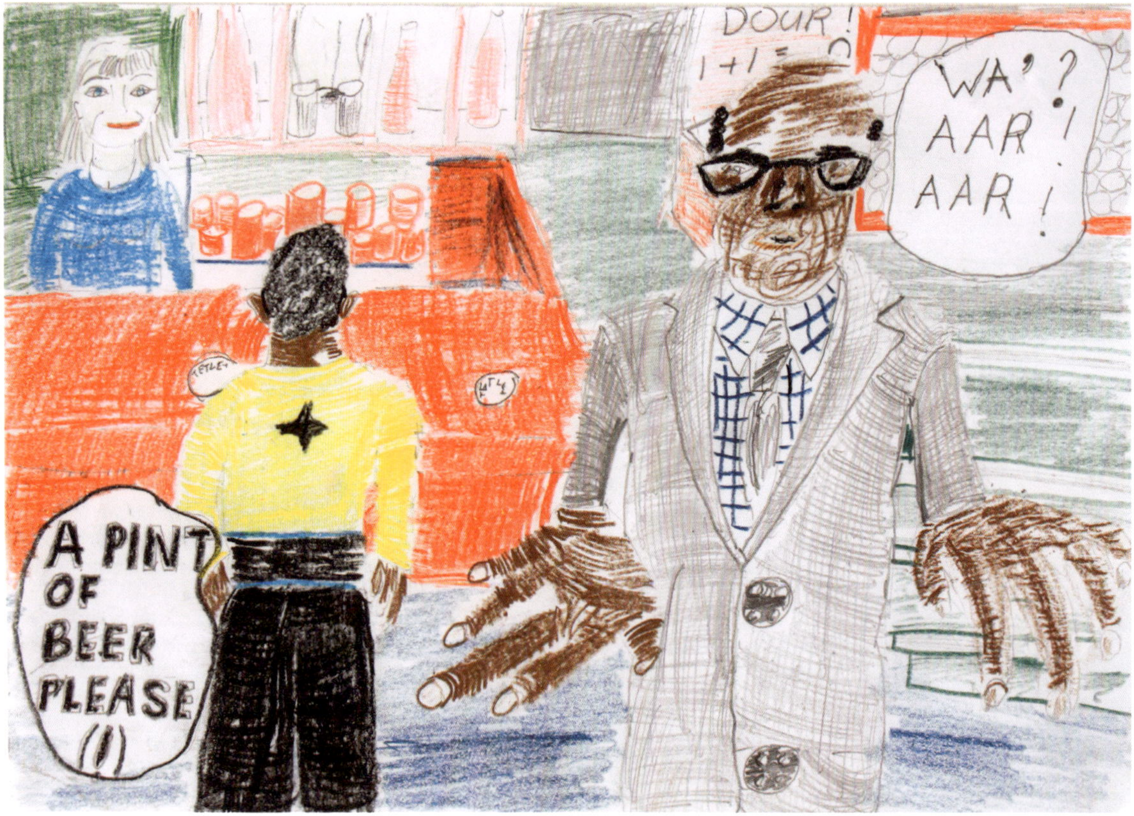
A PINT OF BEER PLEASE (!)
WA'?! AAR! AAR!

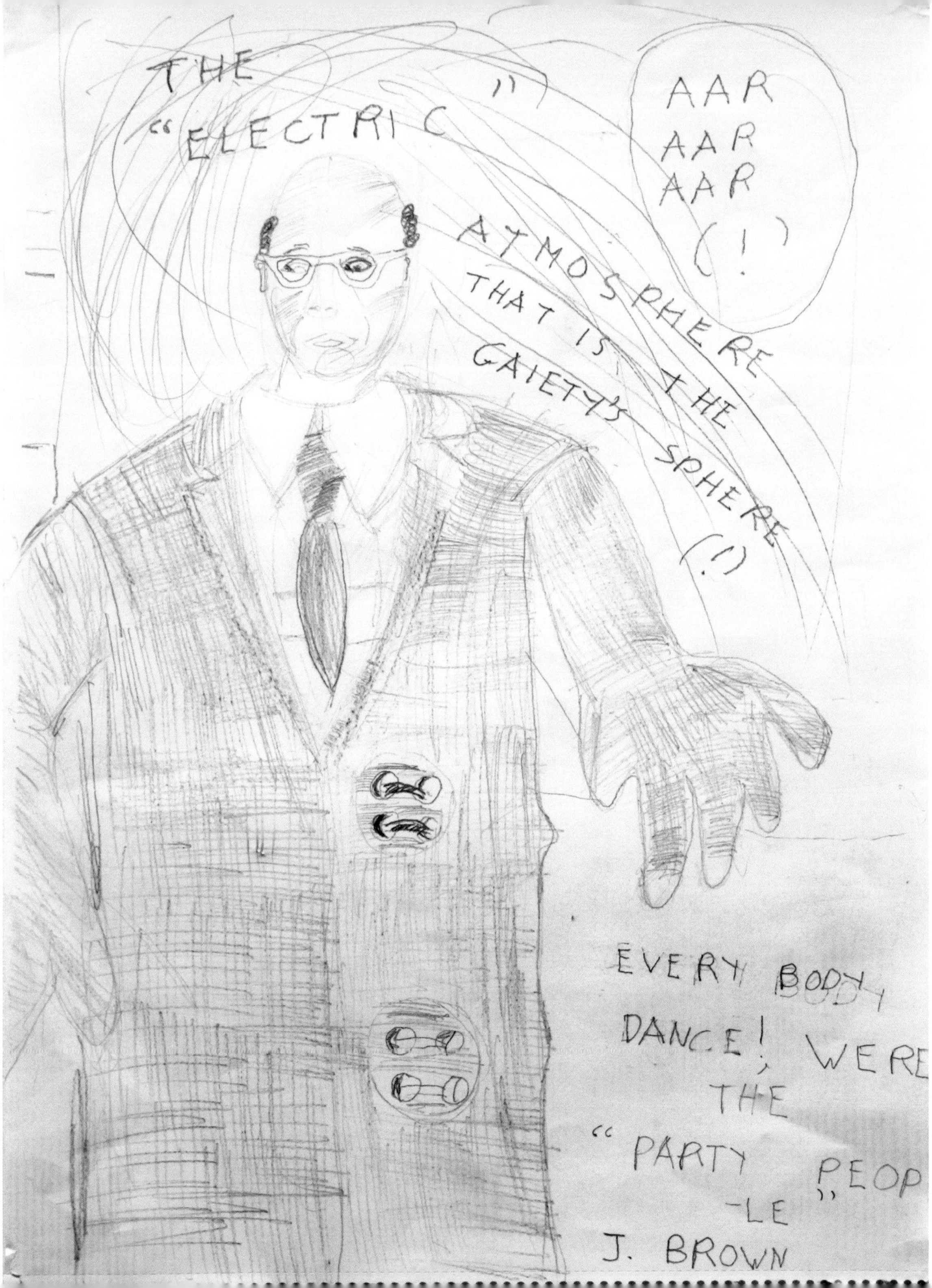
THE "ELECTRIC" ATMOSPHERE THAT IS THE GAIETY'S SPHERE (!)
AAR AAR AAR (!)
EVERY BODY DANCE! WERE THE "PARTY PEOP-LE"
J. BROWN

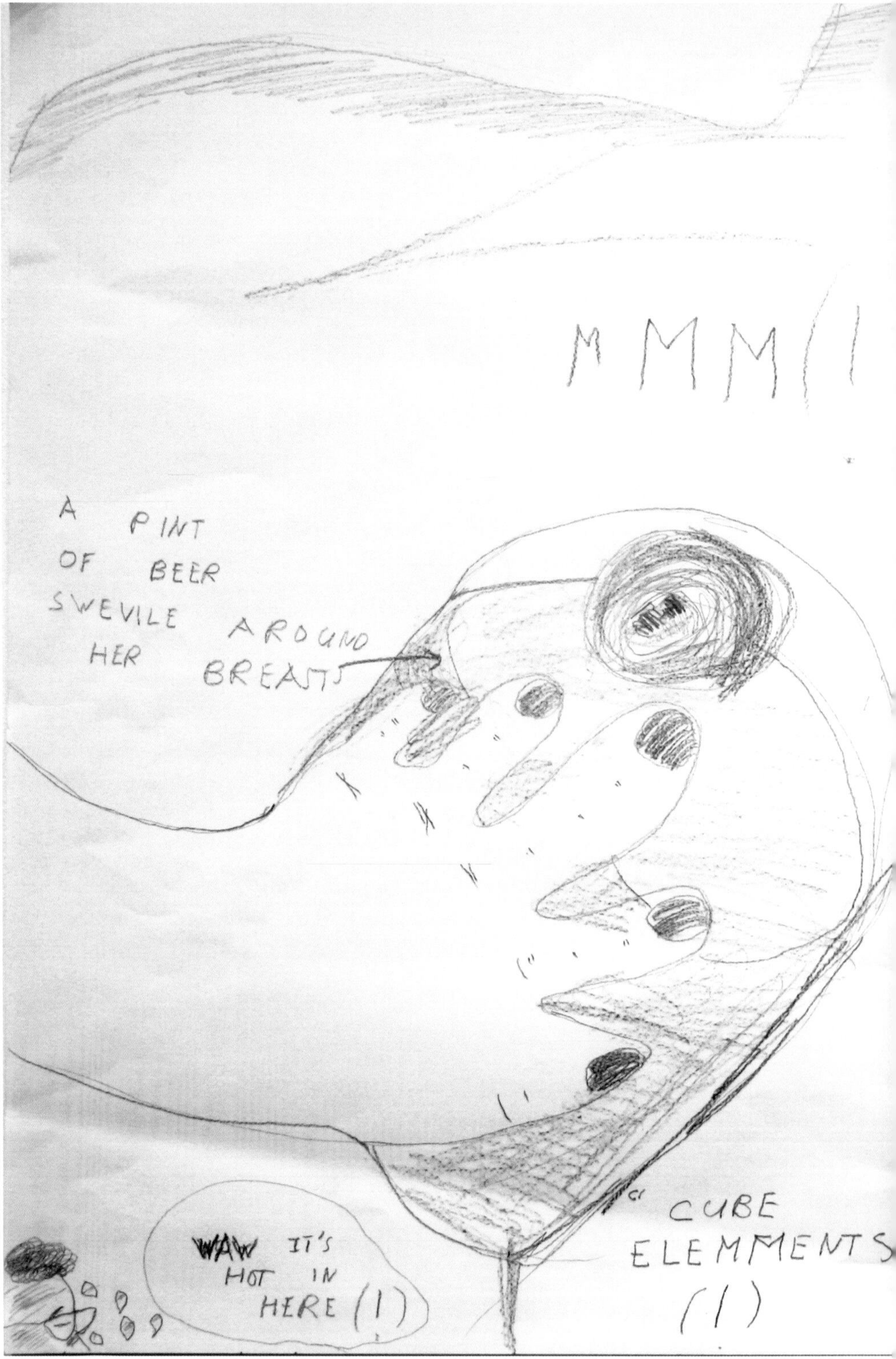
MMM(I
A PINT OF BEER SWEVILE AROUND HER BREASTS
WAW IT'S HOT IN HERE (!)
CUBE ELEMMENTS (!)

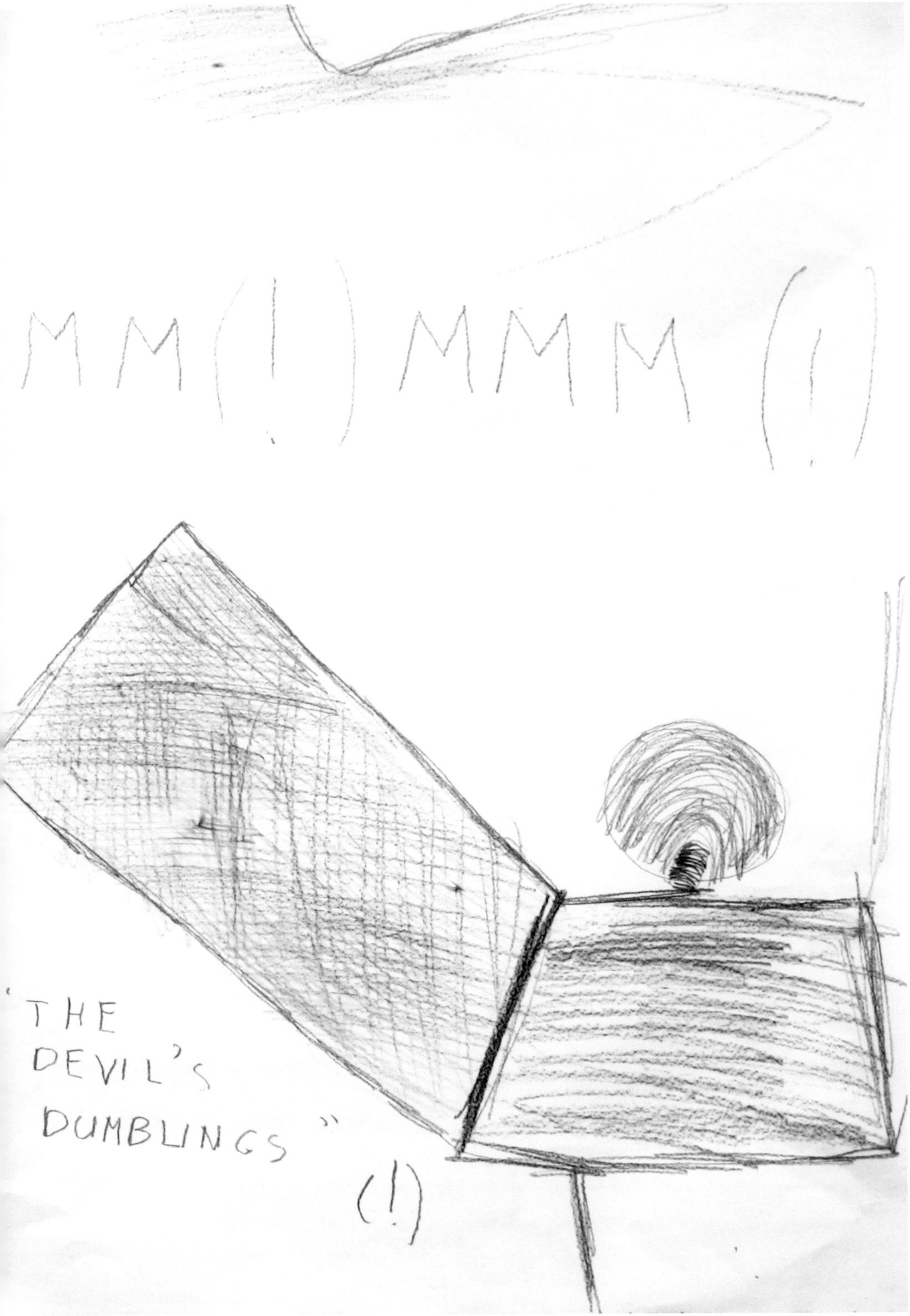
MM(!) MMM(!)
'THE DEVIL'S DUMBLINGS"
(!)

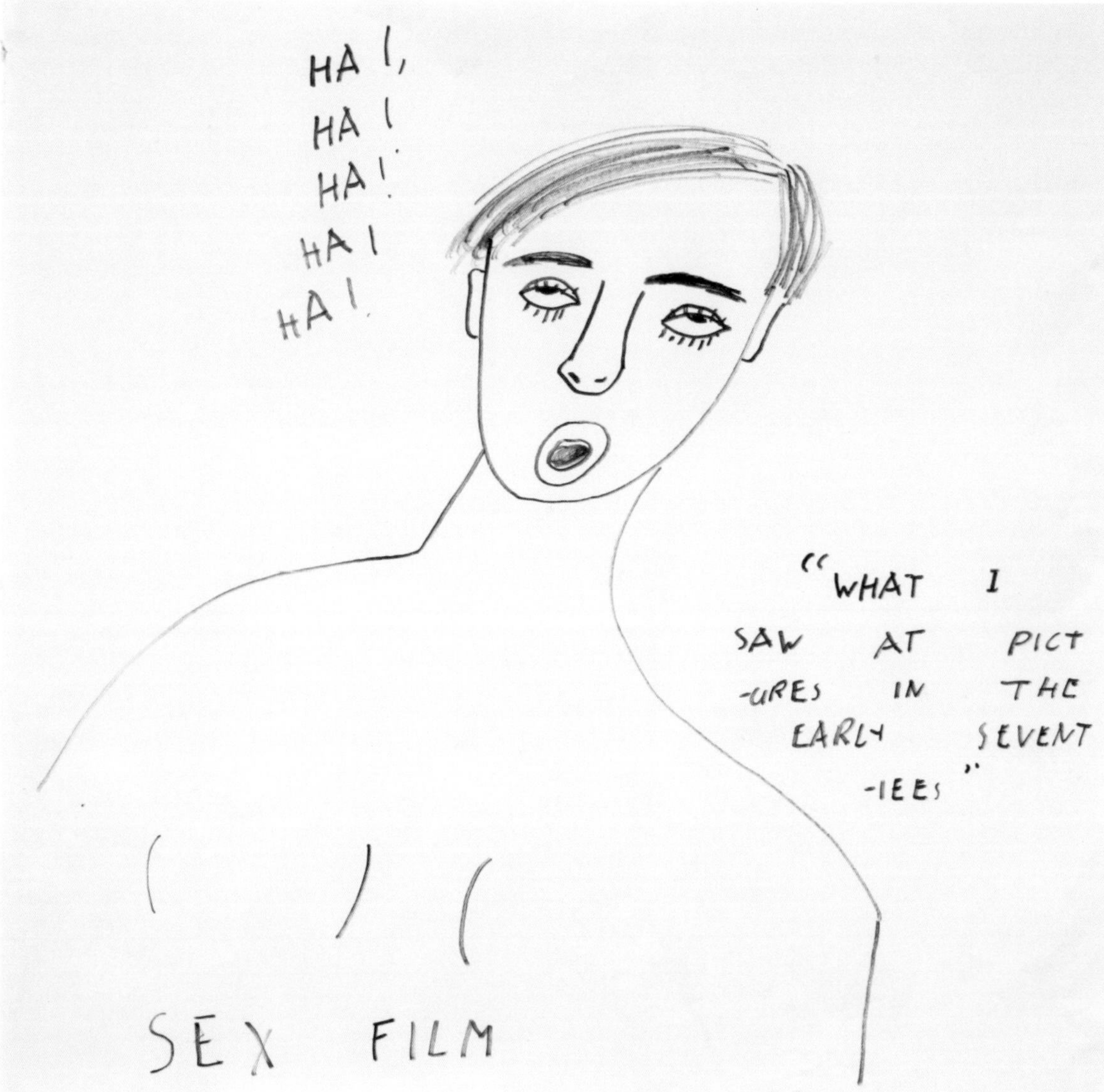
HA!, HA! HA! HA! HA!
"WHAT I SAW AT PICT-URES IN THE EARLY SEVENT-IEES"
SEX FILM

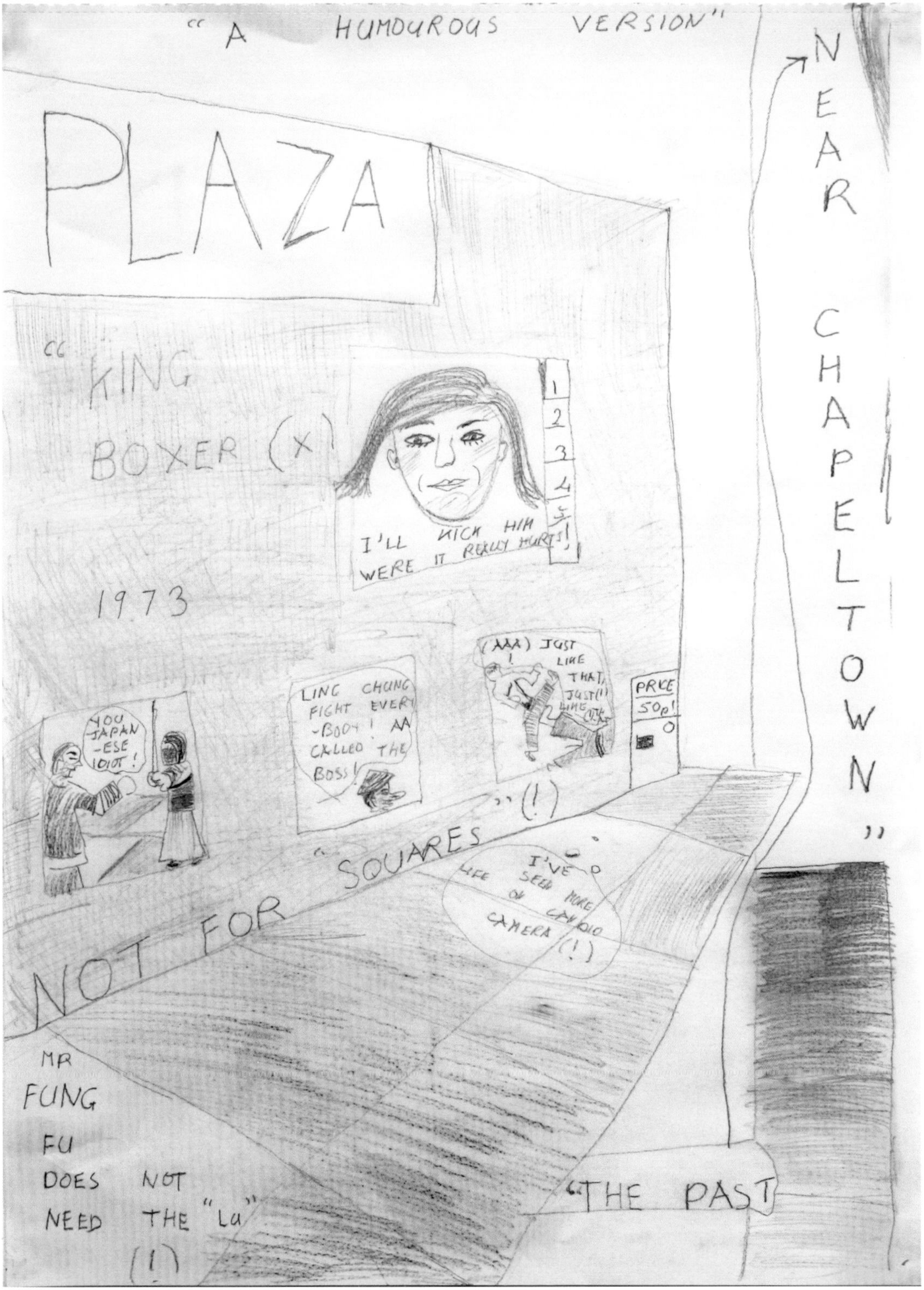
"A HUMOUROUS VERSION"
PLAZA
"KING BOXER (X)
I'LL KICK HIM WERE IT REALLY HURTS!
1 2 3 4 5
1973
YOU JAPAN-ESE IDIOT!
LING CHUNG FIGHT EVERY-BODY! AA CALLED THE BOSS!
(AAA) JUST LIKE THAT, JUST(!)
PRICE 50p!
NOT FOR "SQUARES" (!)
I'VE SEEN MORE LIFE ON CANDID CAMERA (!)
NEAR CHAPELTOWN"
MR FUNG FU DOES NOT NEED THE "Lu" (!)
"THE PAST

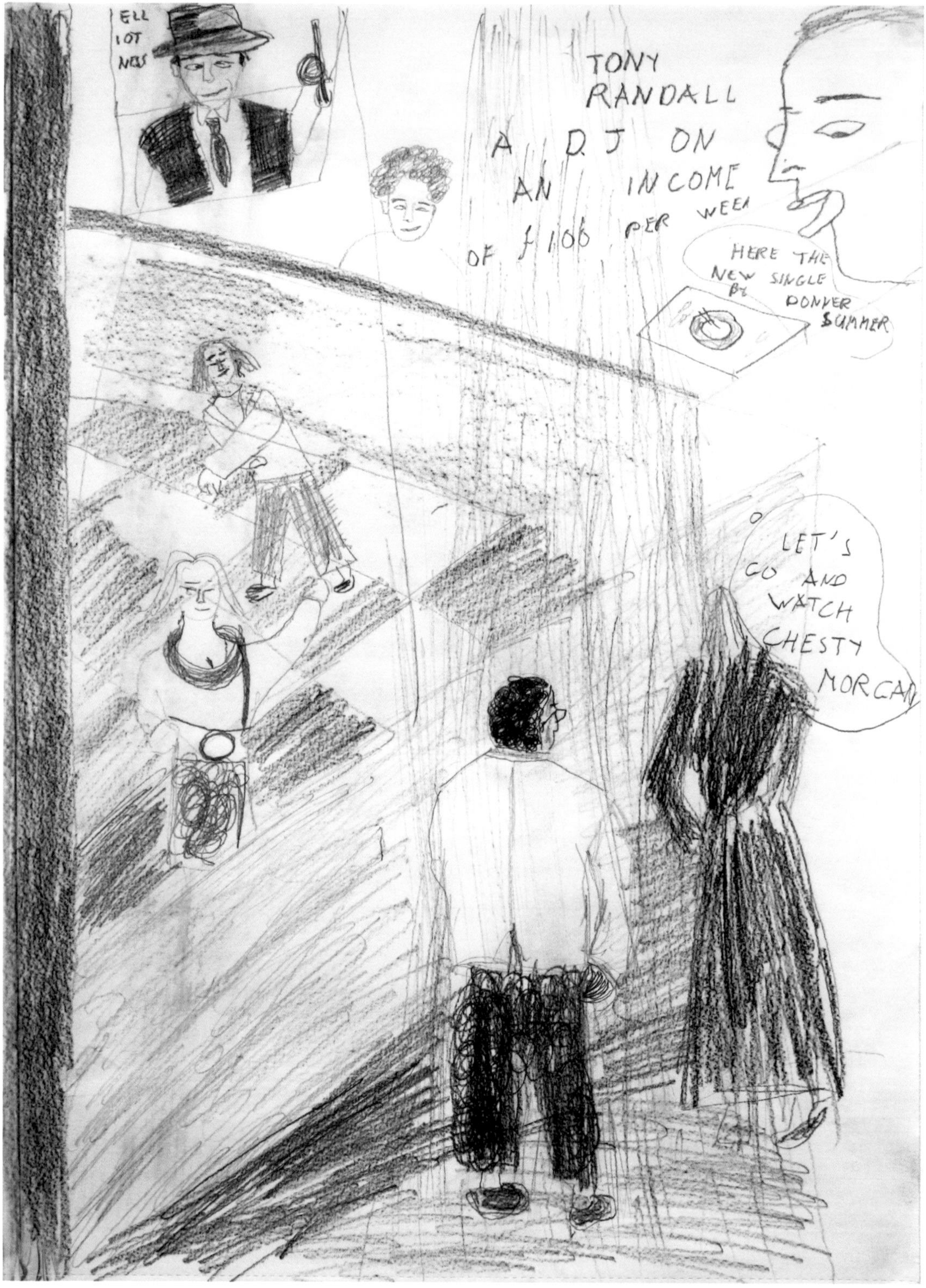
ELL IOT NESS
TONY RANDALL
A D.J ON AN INCOME OF £100 PER WEEK
HERE THE NEW SINGLE BY DONNER SUMMER
LET'S GO AND WATCH CHESTY MORGAN

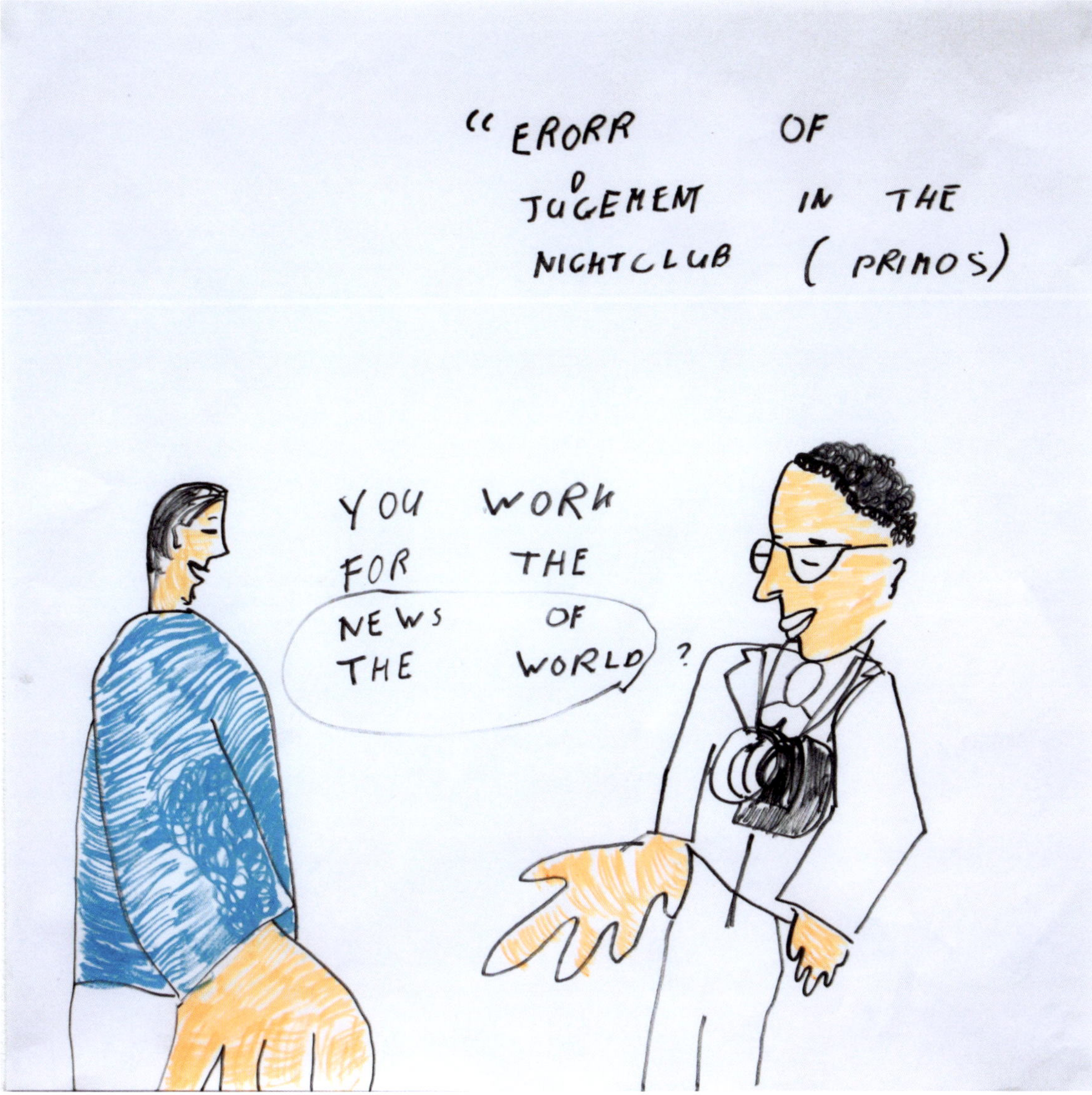
"ERORR OF JUDGEMENT IN THE NIGHTCLUB (PRIMOS)
YOU WORK FOR THE NEWS OF THE WORLD?

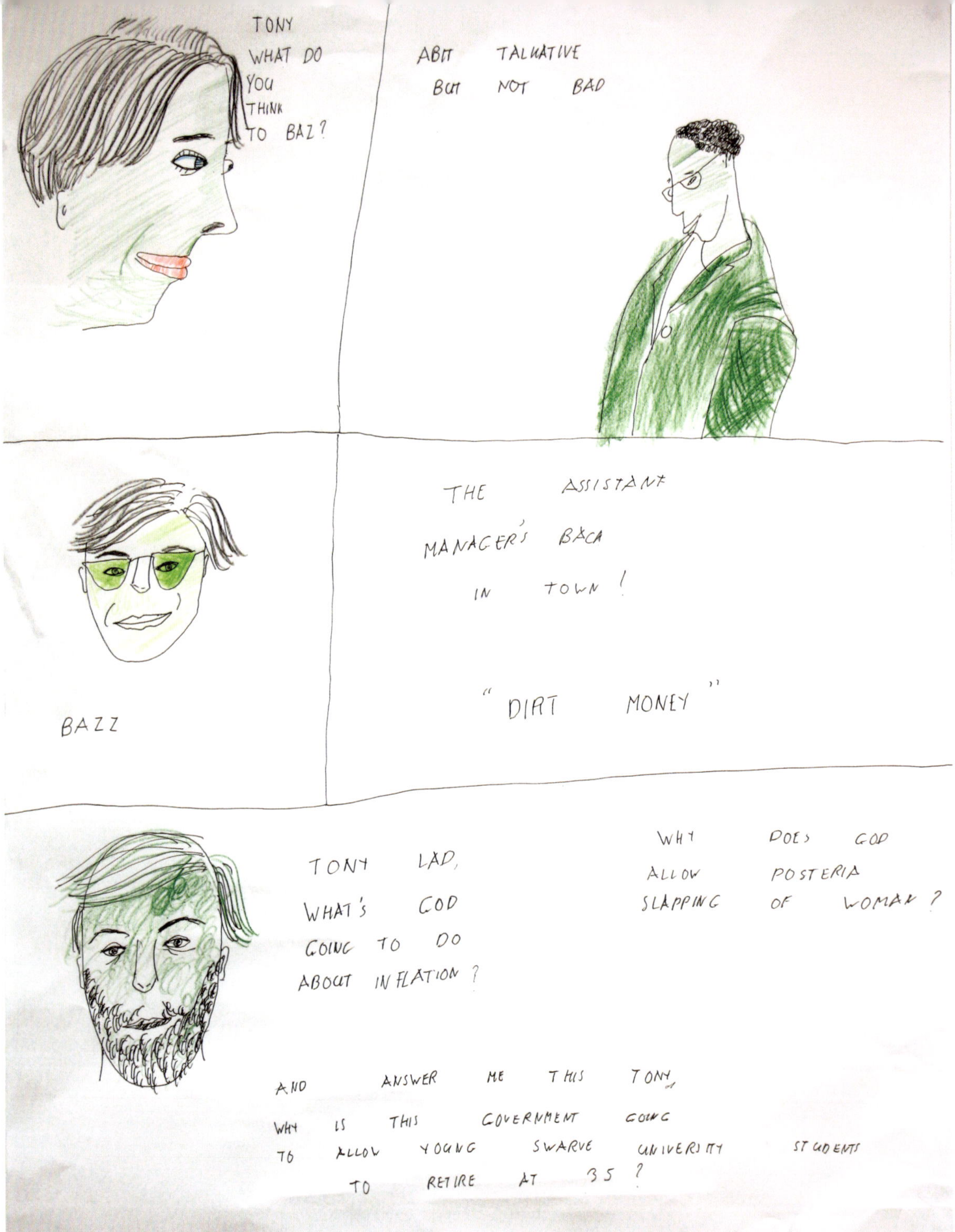

"THE GOSPEL ACCORDING TO RAY ALANS"

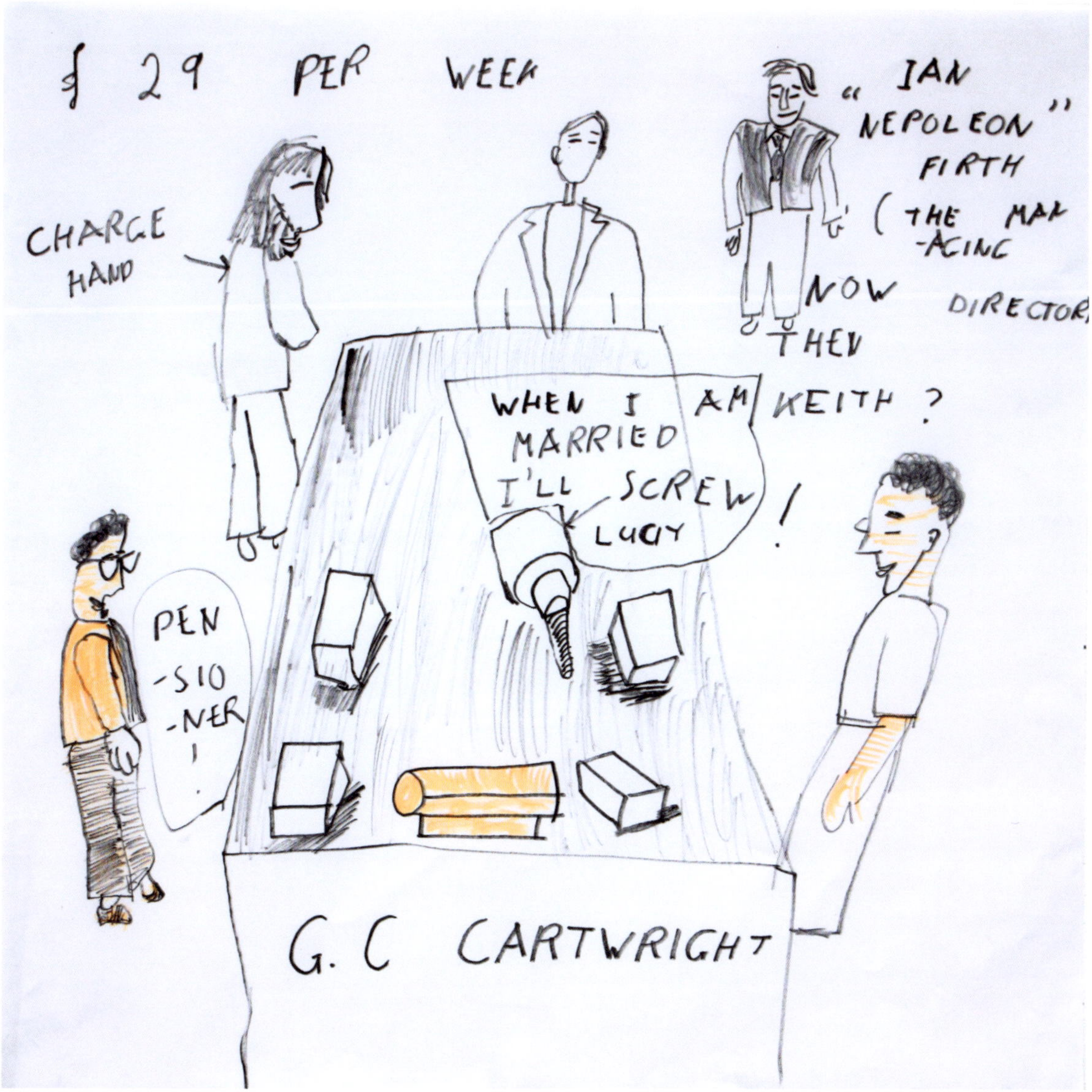
£ 29 PER WEEK
"IAN "NEPOLEON" FIRTH (THE MAN-AGING NOW DIRECTOR THEN
CHARGE HAND
WHEN I AM MARRIED I'LL SCREW LUCY
KEITH ?
!
PEN-SIO-NER !
G. C CARTWRIGHT

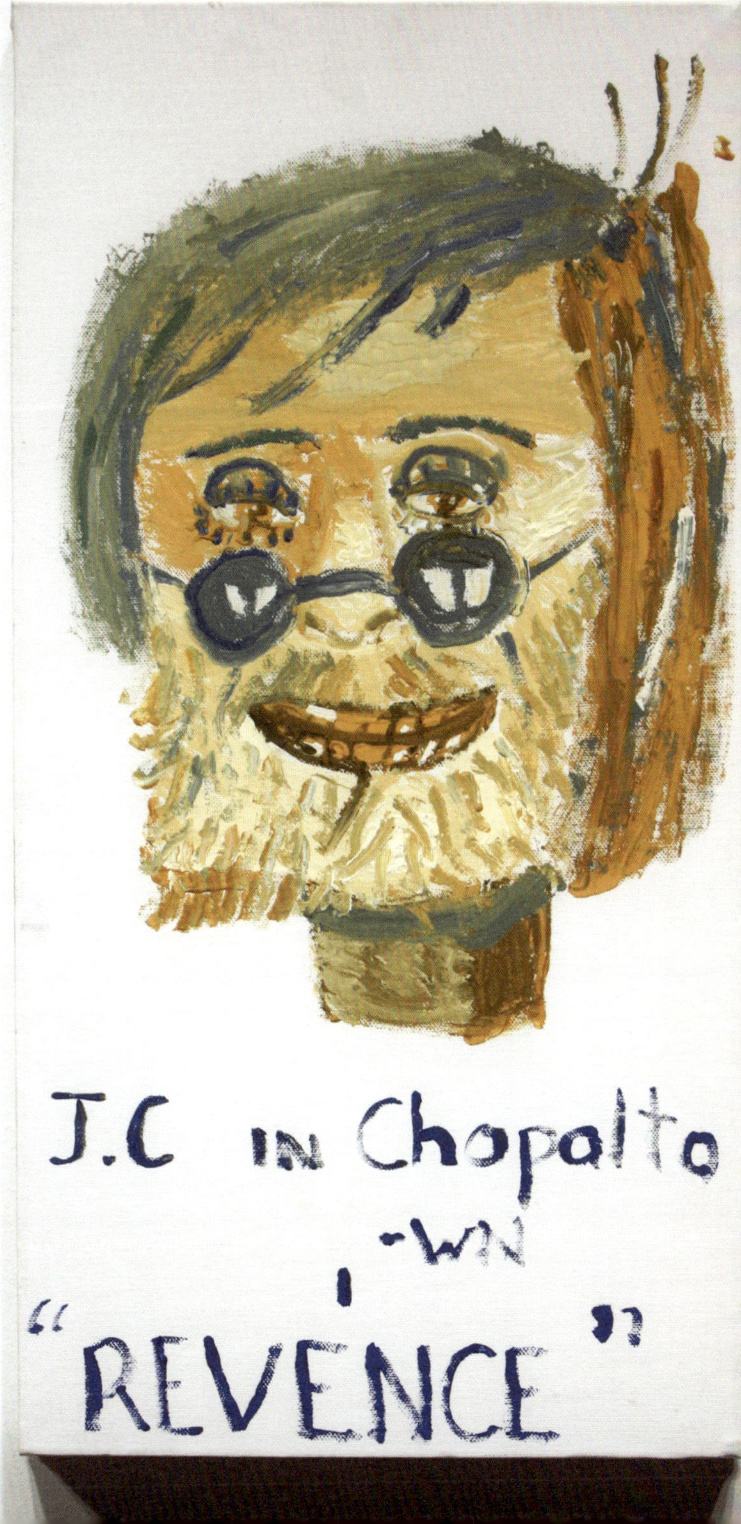
J.C IN Chopalto
"REVENCE"

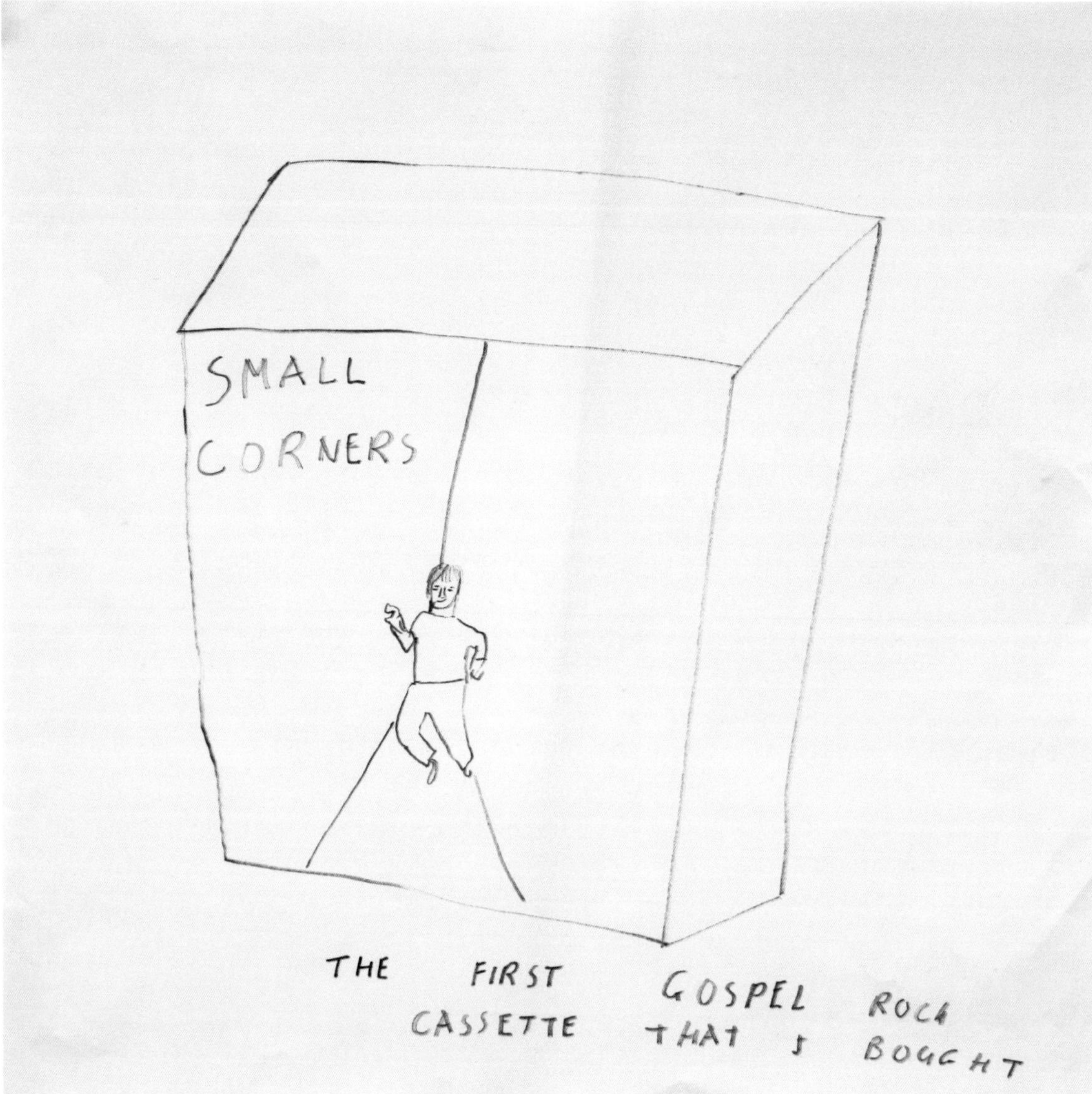
SMALL CORNERS
THE FIRST GOSPEL ROCK CASSETTE THAT I BOUGHT

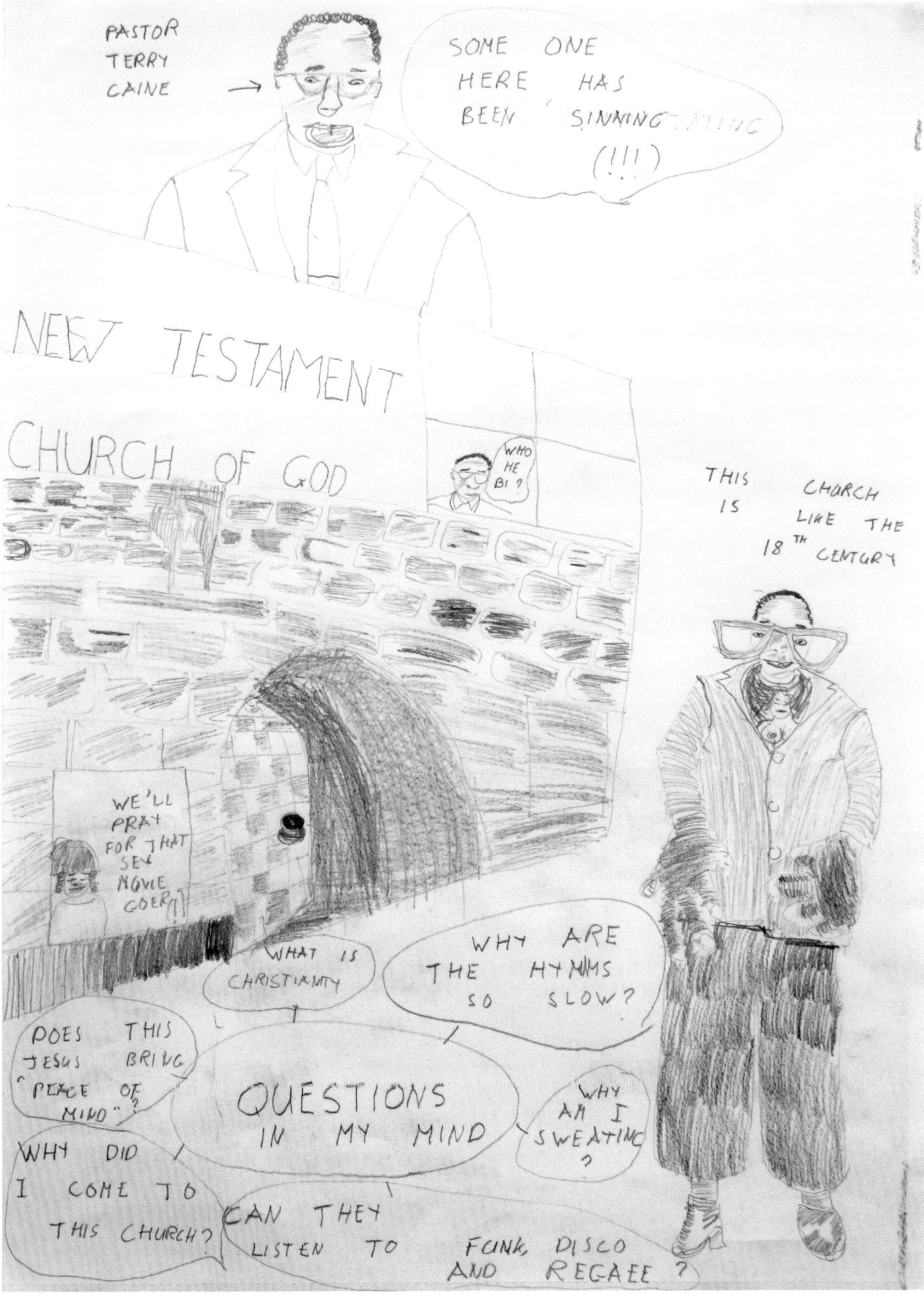
PASTOR TERRY CAINE
SOME ONE HERE HAS BEEN SINNING
(!!!)
NEW TESTAMENT CHURCH OF GOD
WHO HE BI ?
THIS IS CHURCH LIKE THE 18TH CENTURY
WE'LL PRAY FOR THAT SEX MOVIE GOER(!)
WHAT IS CHRISTIANITY
WHY ARE THE HYMNS SO SLOW?
DOES THIS JESUS BRING "PEACE OF MIND"?
QUESTIONS IN MY MIND
WHY AM I SWEATING ?
WHY DID I COME TO THIS CHURCH?
CAN THEY LISTEN TO FUNK, DISCO AND REGAEE ?

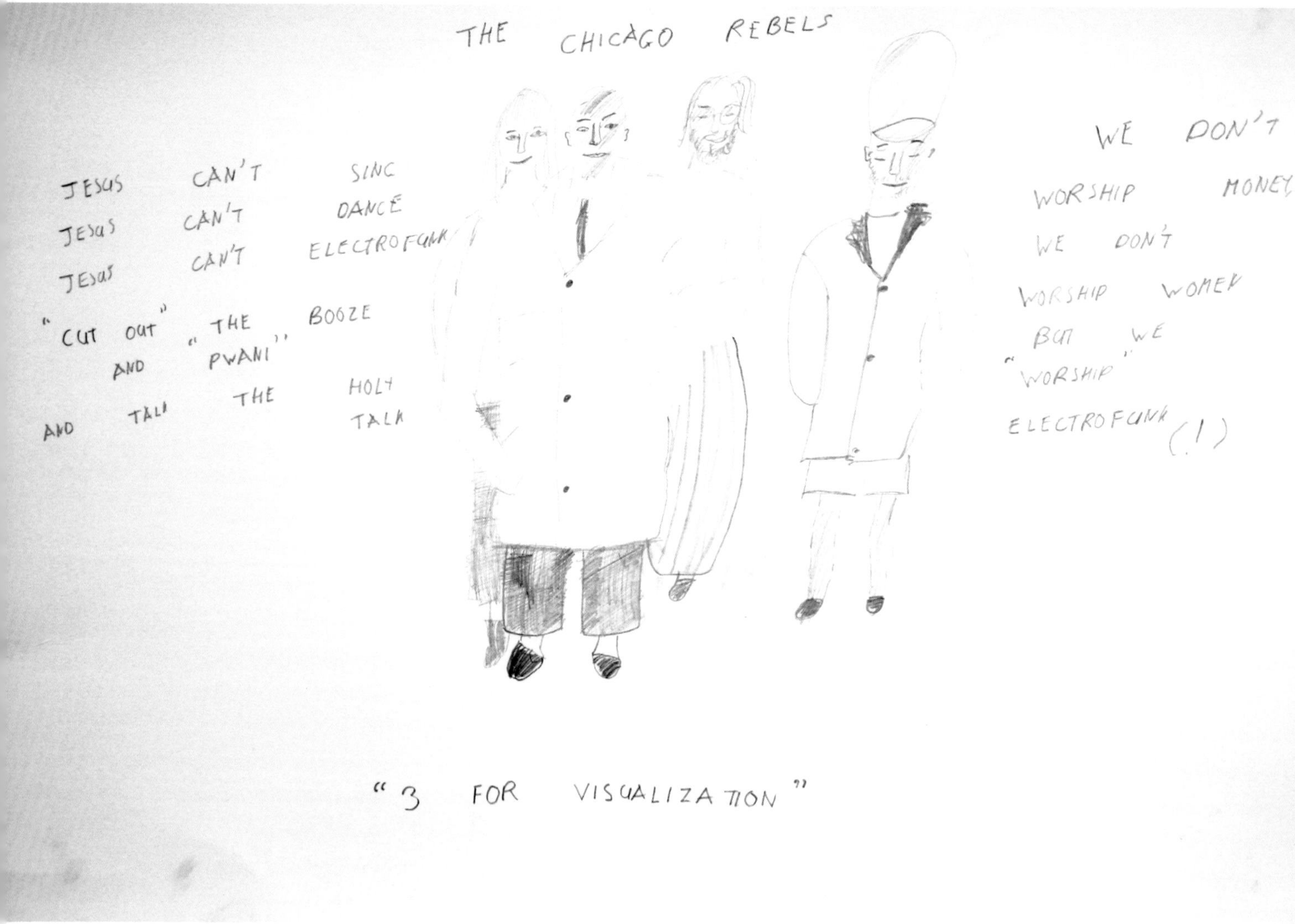
THE CHICAGO REBELS
JESUS CAN'T SING
JESUS CAN'T DANCE
JESUS CAN'T ELECTROFUNK
"CUT OUT" "THE BOOZE
AND "PWANI""
AND TALK THE HOLY TALK
WE DON'T WORSHIP MONEY
WE DON'T WORSHIP WOMEN
BUT WE "WORSHIP" ELECTROFUNK (!)
"3 FOR VISUALIZATION"

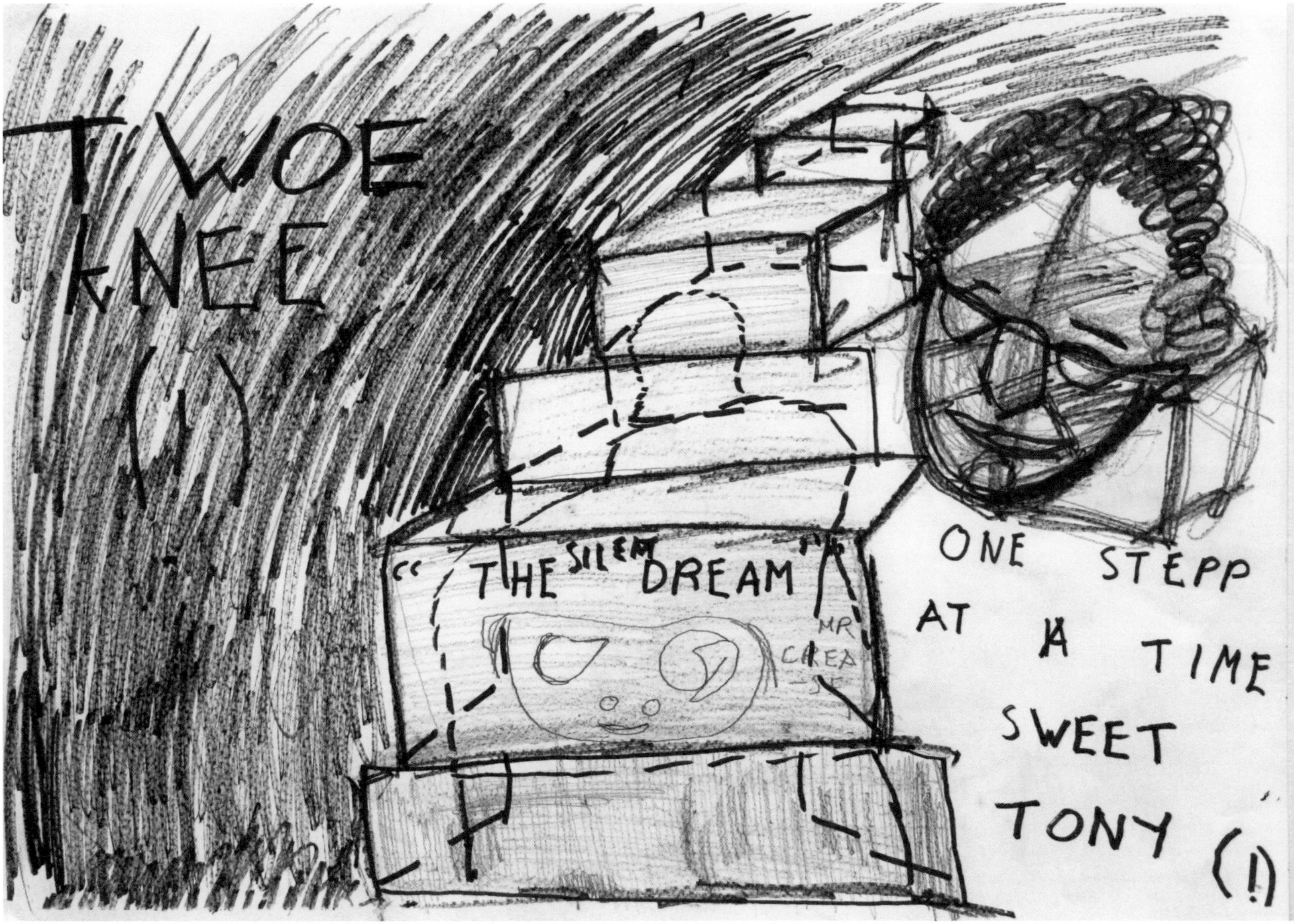
TWOE
KNEE
(!)
"THE SILENT DREAM"
MR
CREA
-SE
ONE STEPP
AT A TIME
SWEET
TONY (!)

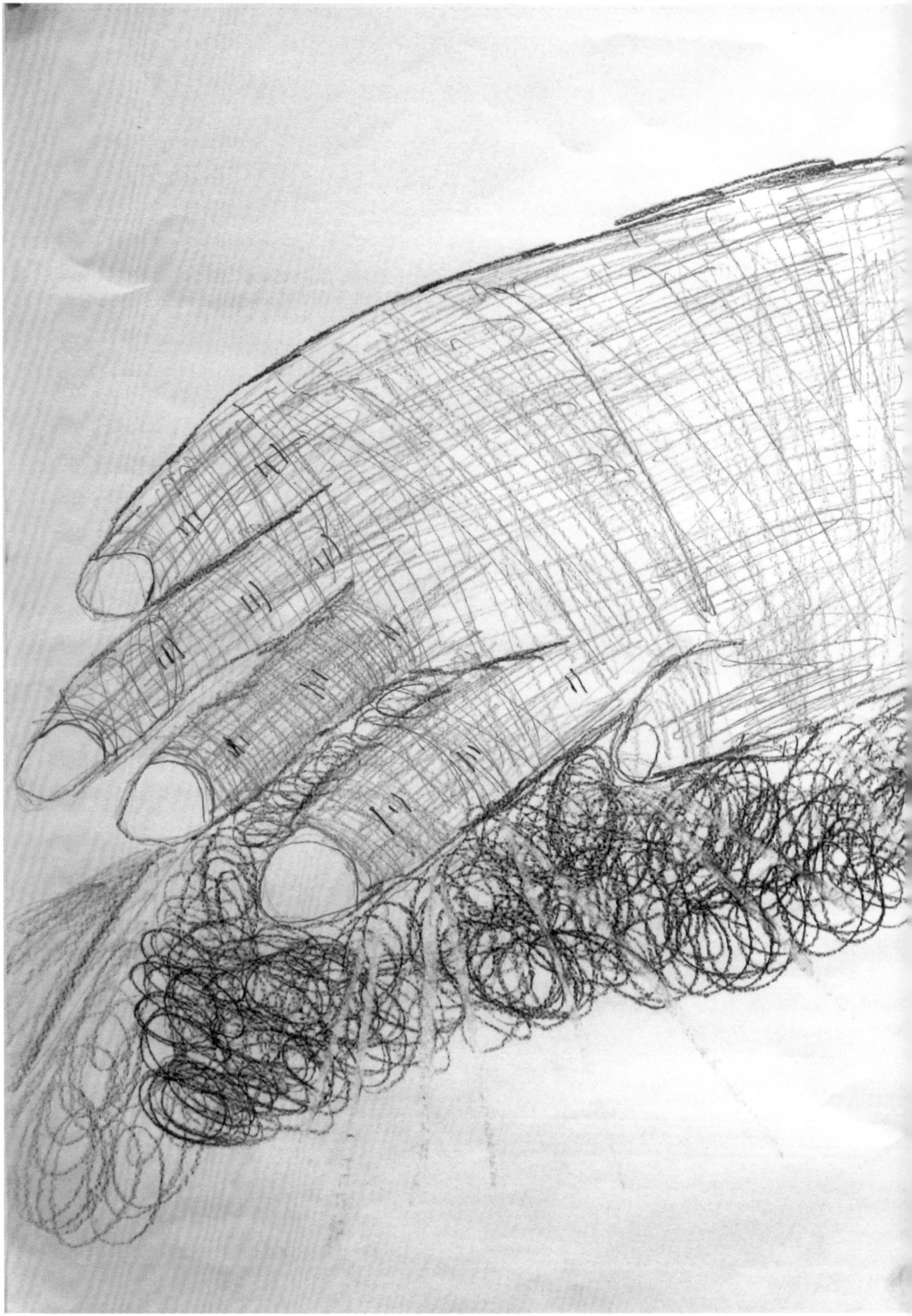

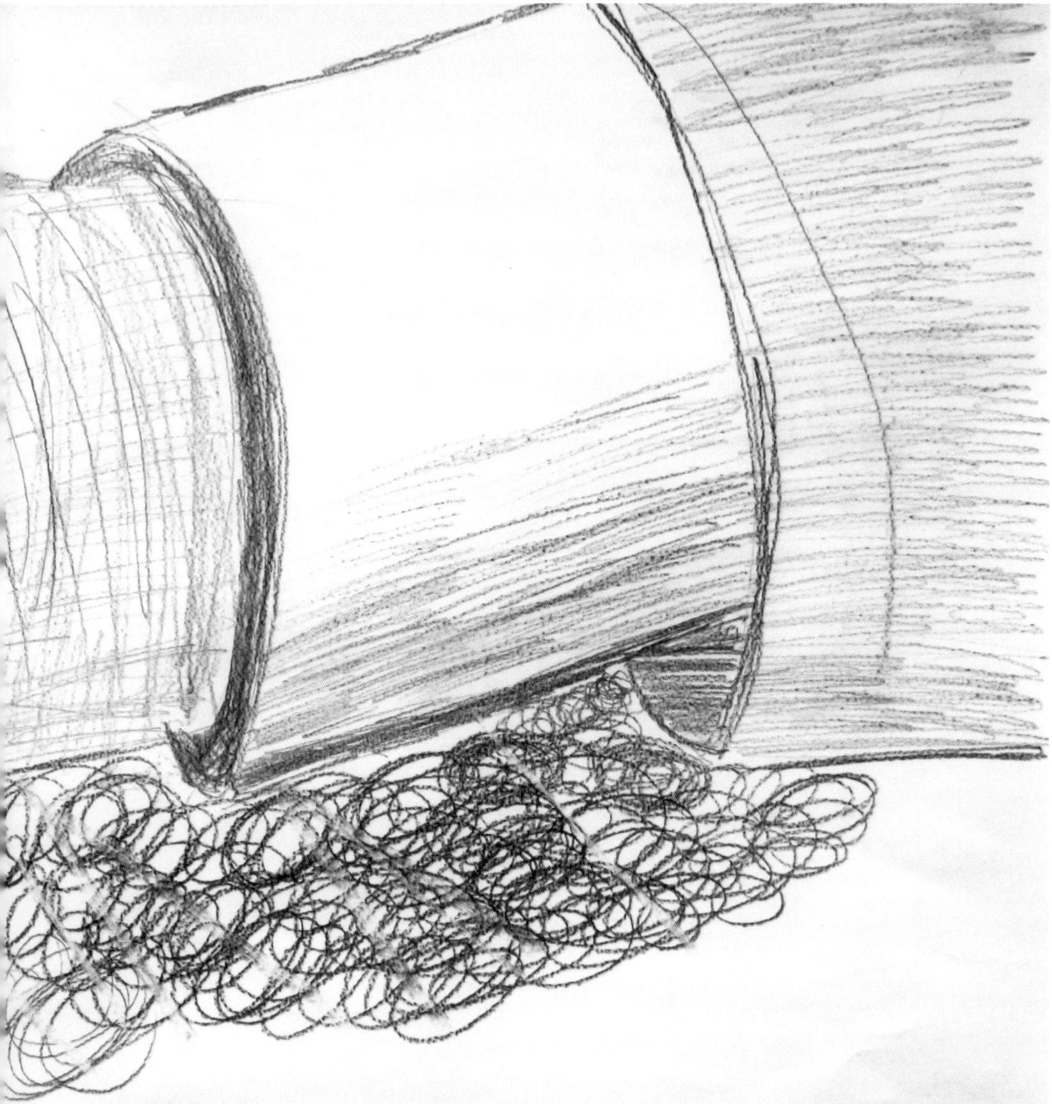

"SEE THE LIGHT"

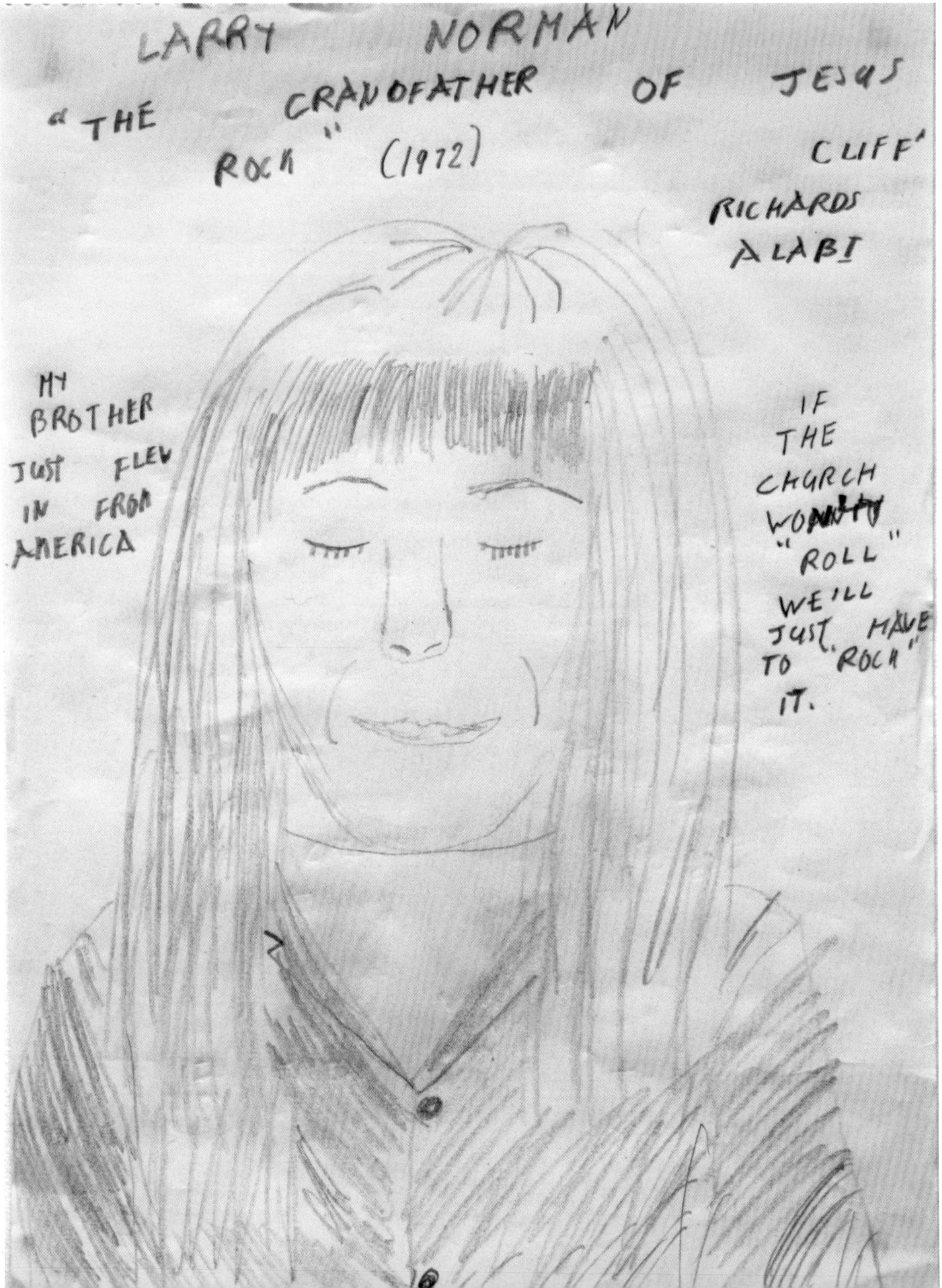
LARRY NORMAN
"THE GRANDFATHER OF JESUS ROCK" (1972)
CLIFF' RICHARDS ALABI
MY BROTHER JUST FLEW IN FROM AMERICA
IF THE CHURCH WON'T "ROLL" WE'LL JUST HAVE TO "ROCK" IT.

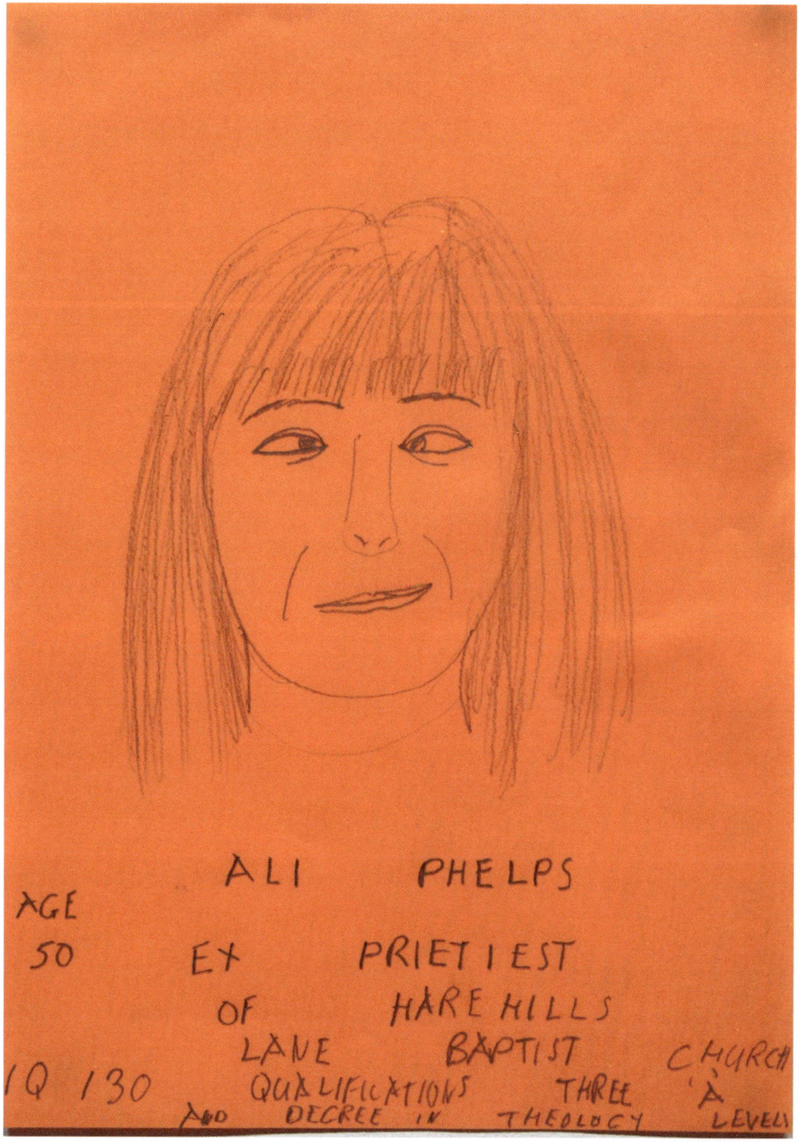
ALI PHELPS
AGE
50 EX PRIETIEST
OF HARE HILLS
LANE BAPTIST CHURCH
IQ 130 QUALIFICATIONS THREE 'A'
AND DECREE IN THEOLOGY LEVELS

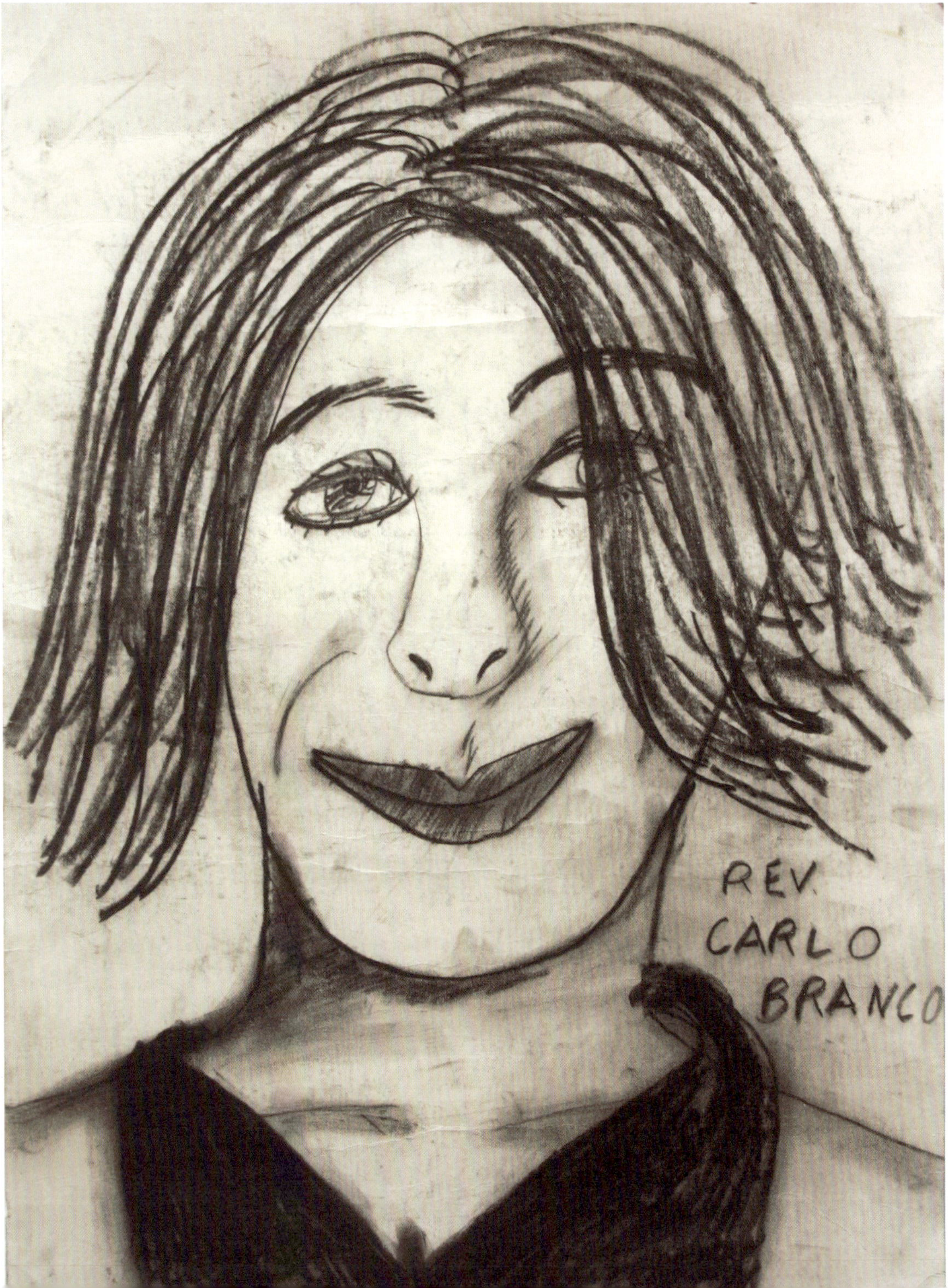
REV.
CARLO
BRANCO

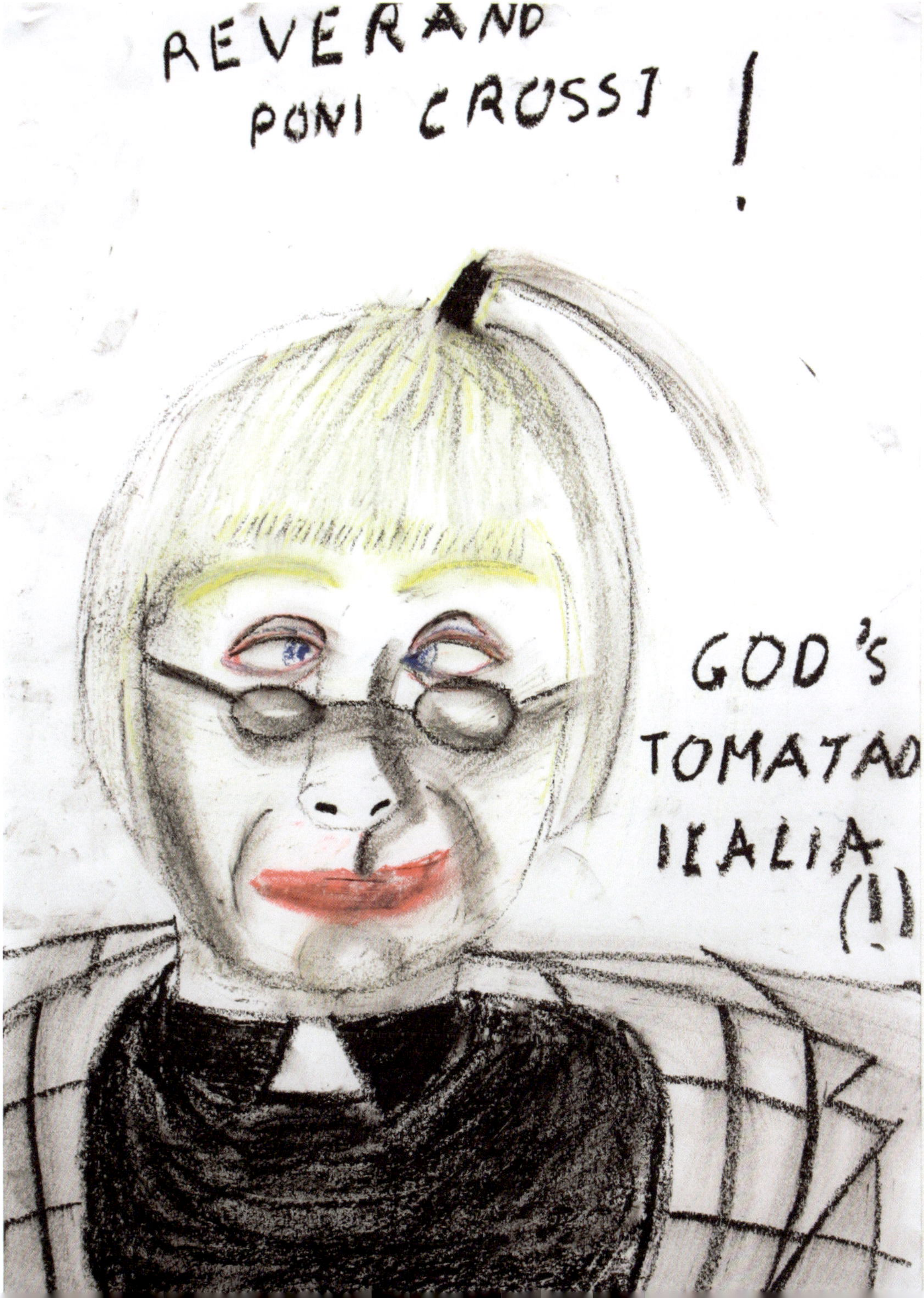
REVERAND PONI CROSSI !
GOD'S TOMATAO ITALIA (!)

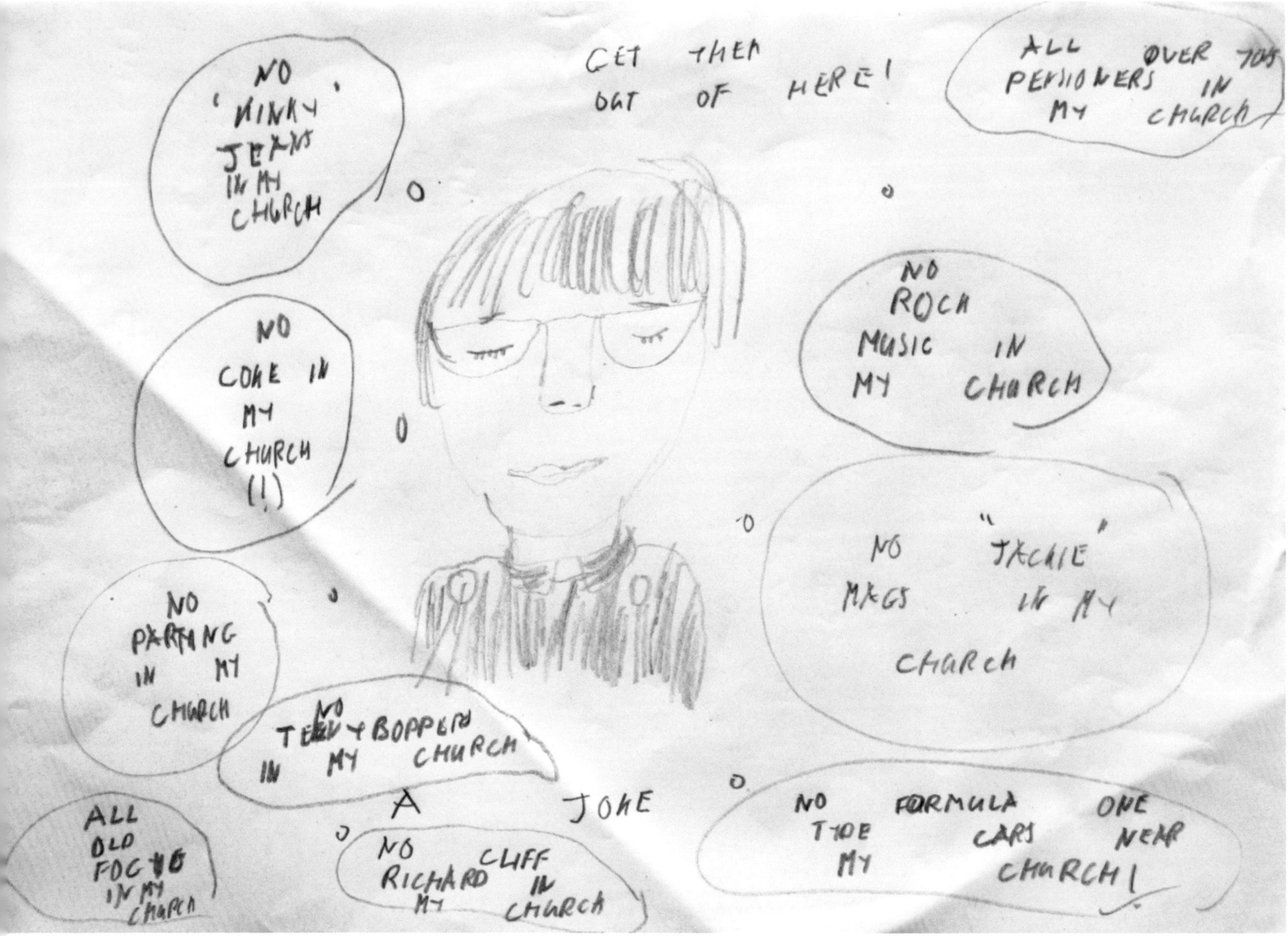
NO 'KINKY' JEANS IN MY CHURCH
GET THEM OUT OF HERE!
ALL OVER 70S PENSIONERS IN MY CHURCH!
NO COKE IN MY CHURCH (!)
NO ROCK MUSIC IN MY CHURCH
NO "JACKIE" MAGS IN MY CHURCH
NO PARKING IN MY CHURCH
NO TEENYBOPPERS IN MY CHURCH
A JOKE
ALL OLD FOGIES IN MY CHURCH
NO CLIFF RICHARD IN MY CHURCH
NO FORMULA ONE TYPE CARS NEAR MY CHURCH!

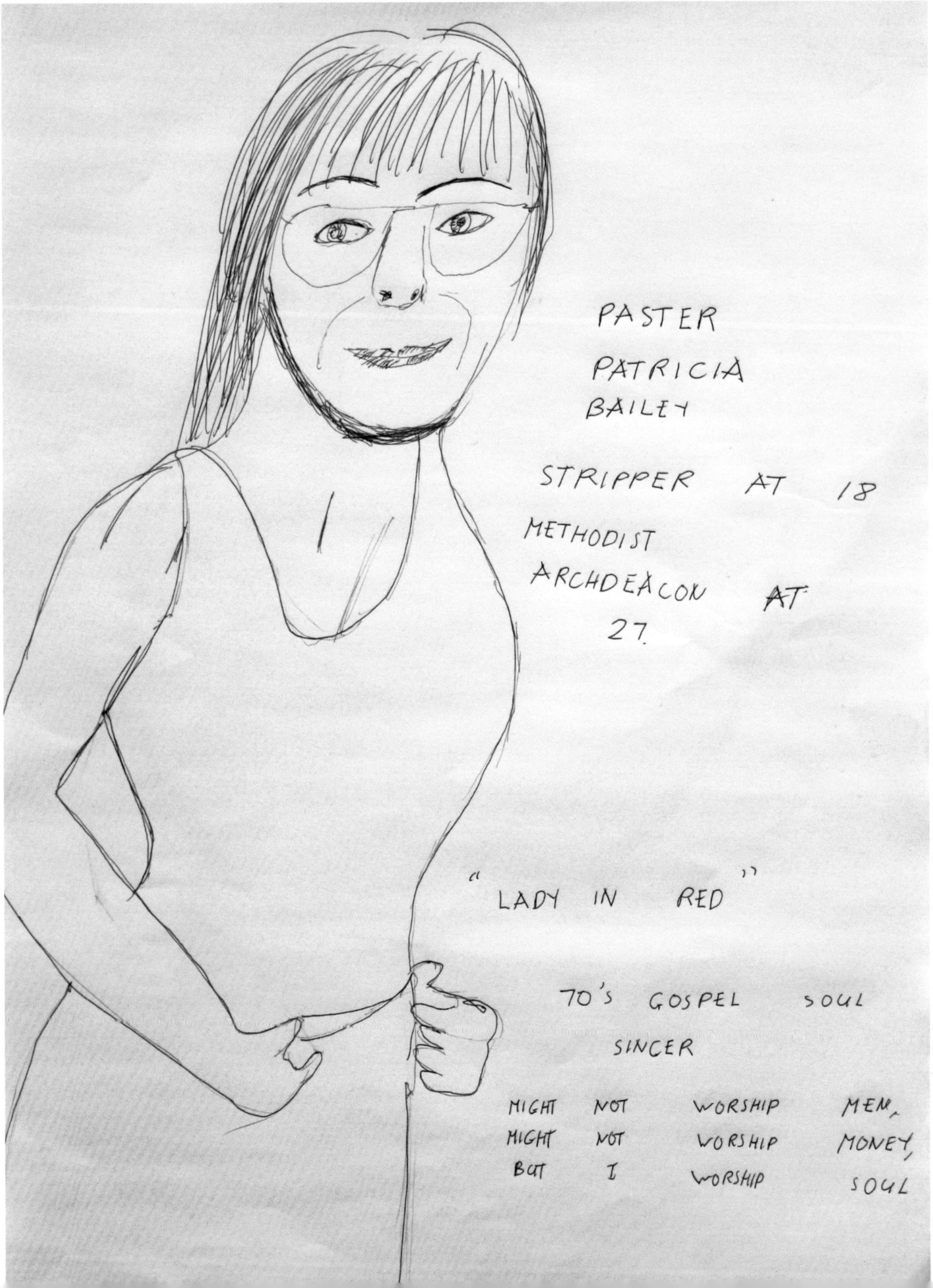
PASTER
PATRICIA
BAILEY
STRIPPER AT 18
METHODIST
ARCHDEACON AT
27.
"LADY IN RED"
70'S GOSPEL SOUL
SINCER
MIGHT NOT WORSHIP MEN,
MIGHT NOT WORSHIP MONEY,
BUT I WORSHIP SOUL

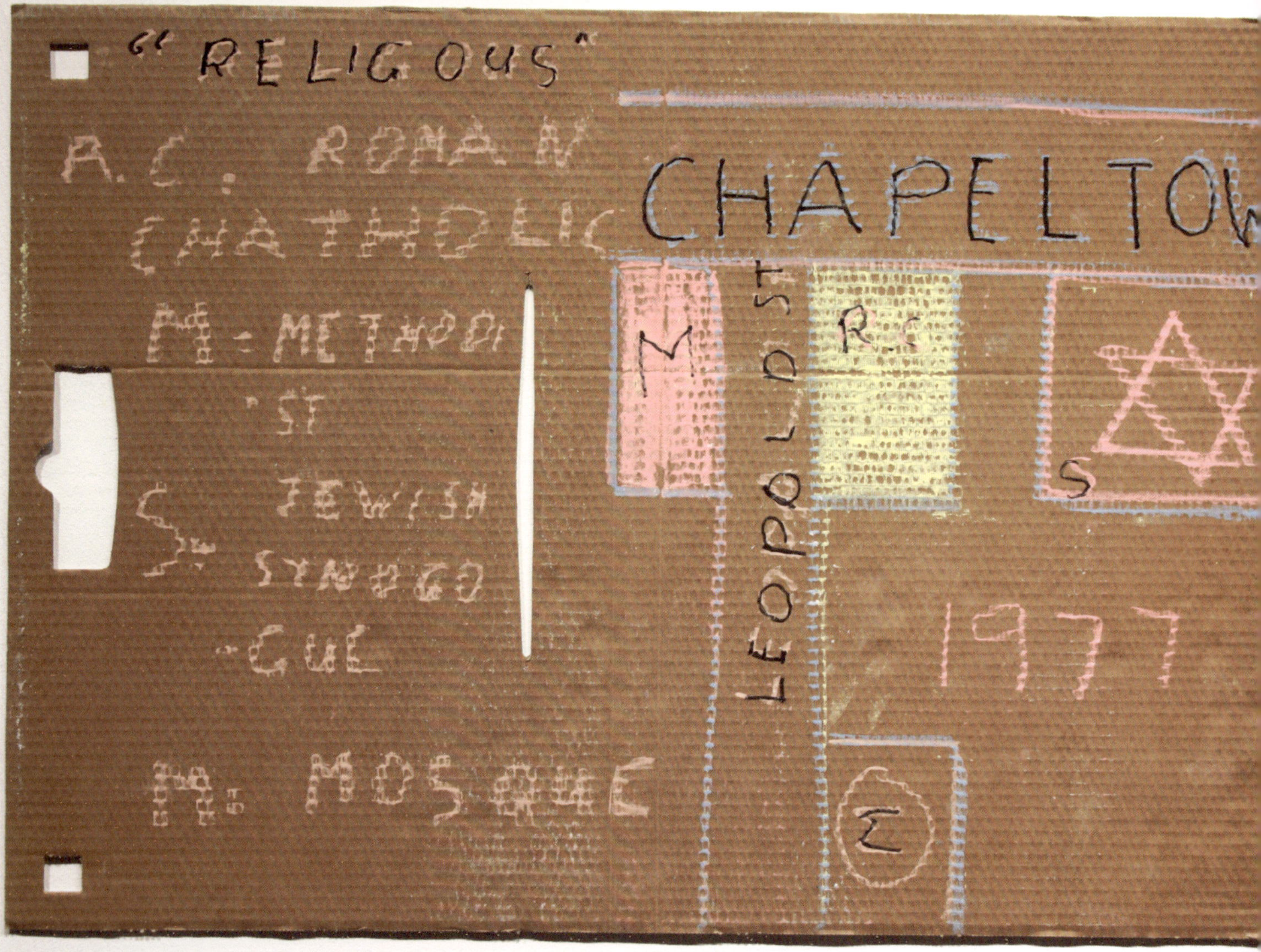
"RELIGOUS"
R.C. ROMAN
CHATHOLIC
M - METHODI
ST
S - JEWISH
SYNOGO
-GUE
M - MOSQUE
CHAPELTOW
LEOPOLD ST
M
R.C
S
1977

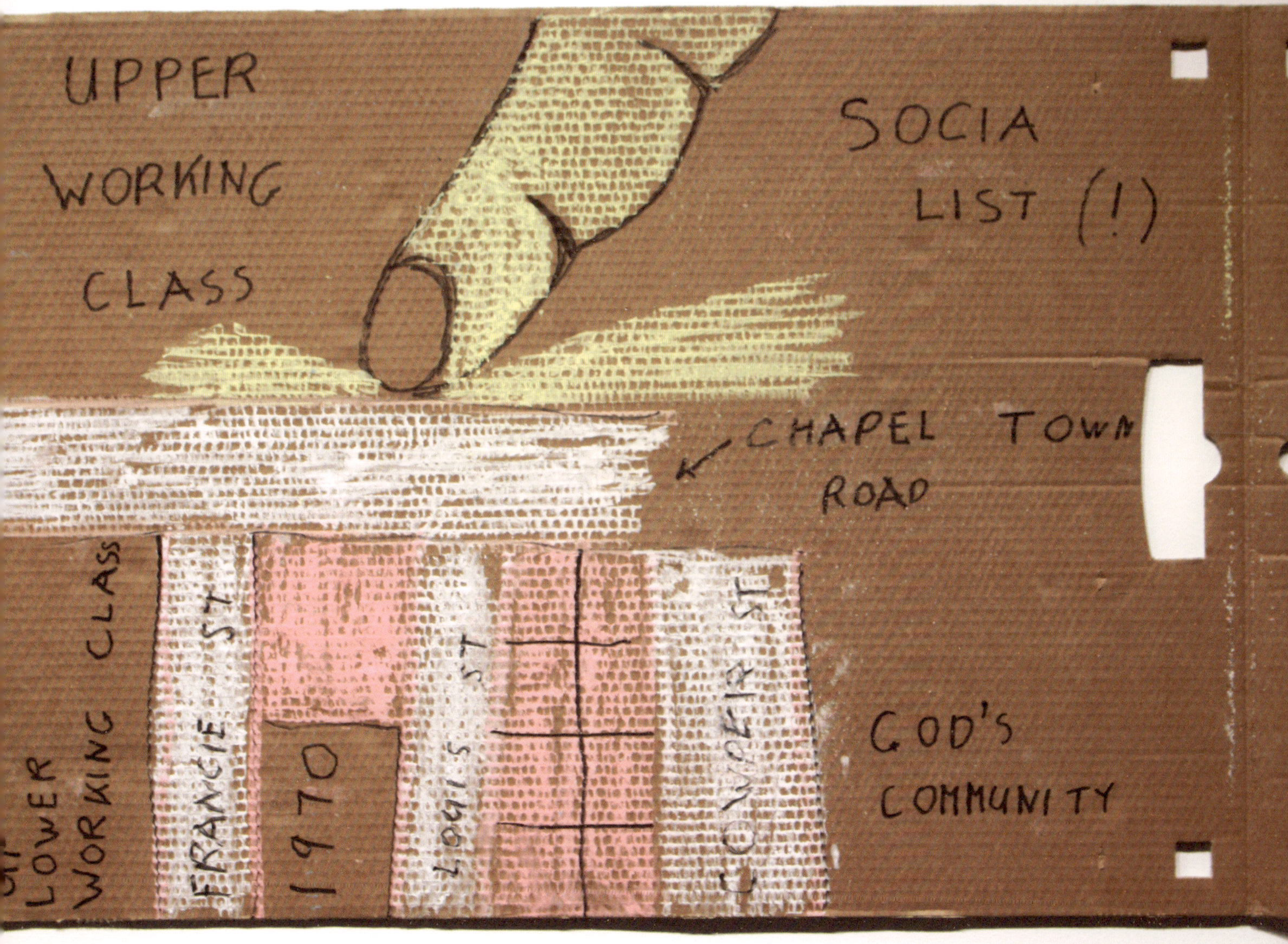
UPPER
WORKING
CLASS
SOCIA
LIST (!)
CHAPEL TOWN
ROAD
LOWER
WORKING CLASS
FRANCIS ST
1970
LOUIS ST
COWPER ST
GOD'S
COMMUNITY

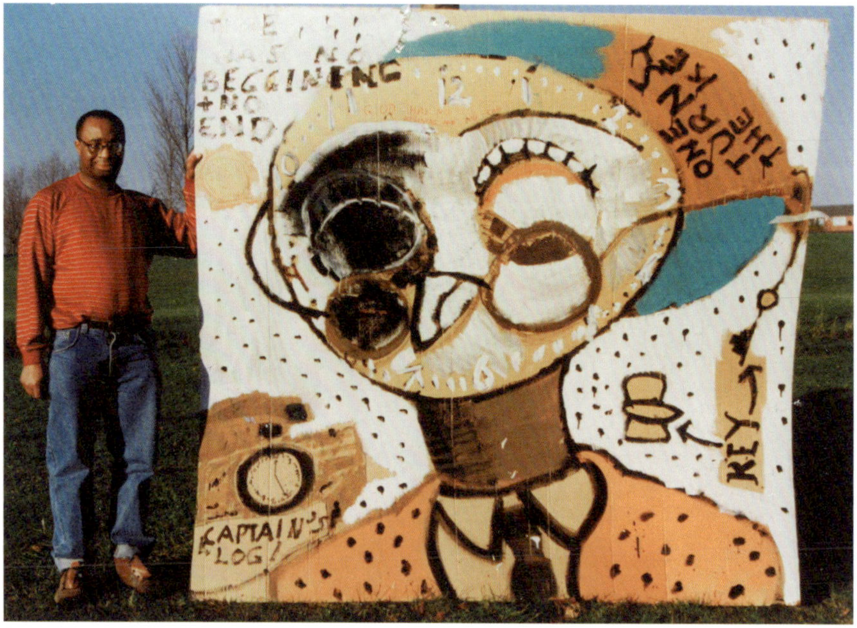

Tony Tomlin, Thomas Danby College 1996

Image credits

Tony Tomlin with 'Jesus Goes to Berlin for Hardcore Music' : Jon Wakeman

Tony Tomlin with 'Socialist at My Door' : Dave Peel

Tony Tomlin with 'Captain's Log!' : Kevin O'Hare

Tony Tomlin and Jon Wakeman at Union 105: Tim Smith

Tony Tomlin waiting to be shaved : Dave Peel